KU-717-470

WITHDRAWN
FROM STOCK

Colaiste Oideachais Mhuire Gan Smal
Luimneach

THE IRISH TOWN
an approach to survival

255

First Published 1975
The O'Brien Press
11 Clare Street Dublin 2 Ireland

O'BRIEN PRESS:
ISBN: 9502046 5 X (Standard Ed.)
ISBN: 9502046 6 8 (Special Ed.)

Copyright
©Patrick Shaffrey
and The O'Brien Press

All rights reserved. No part of this book
may be reproduced or utilised in any
form or by any means, electronic or
mechanical, including photocopying, recording
or by any information storage and
retrieval system without permission
in writing from the publisher.

Coláiste Oideachais
Mhuire Gan Smál
Luimneach
Class No. 301·3609415 SHA
Acc. No. 25620

Cover Design by Michael O'Brien
Printed by E. & T. O'Brien Ltd. 11 Clare Street
Dublin 2. Ireland.
Typesetting by Actis and the printers
Bound in Dublin by J.F. Newman (standard Edition)
and Museum Bookbinding (Special Limited Edition)

THE IRISH TOWN

an approach to survival

Patrick Shaffrey

THE O'BRIEN PRESS
11 CLARE STREET DUBLIN 2 IRELAND

2550

Contents

About this book

This is not a book about preservation. It does not consider towns as mere museum pieces. It accepts and welcomes the need for new developments, but attempts to show how development can take place without destroying the character and quality of our towns and villages throughout the country. Generally it is concerned with the 'small architecture' which is to be found all over the country. In other words, the house next door, or the shop across the street, buildings which constitute the vast bulk of our architectural heritage. They are subject to all sorts of pressures. They were built by, and are still being used by ordinary people.

This, however, does not mean that the grand architecture of castles, churches, georgian houses is not relevant. By and large the importance of these buildings is widely appreciated, although many are subject to pressures and dangers of various kinds.

In a book of this sort it is difficult to assess and comment on various problems in an objective manner without being specific. Many points are illustrated by examples from all over the country, and are arranged in such a way so as to be easily understood by the general reader. All the examples are from Ireland, and this demonstrates that while we have the capacity to destroy the architectural character of our towns, we do also have the skill, imagination and abilities to develop our towns in an attractive and highly individualistic 'Irish manner'. We have inherited a fine tradition from past generations, and we now hold this in trust for future generations. During our stewardship our towns will change and develop in many ways. How we direct these changes is our responsibility.

This book represents a personal view of the problems which will arise out of these changes. It does not in any way attempt to reflect the views of the organisations or individuals who have supported the book. The opinions, faults, omissions are entirely my own.

I hope, however, the book will make people aware of the character of our towns; of the 'Irishness' to be found in both North and South. This makes them different, but not necessarily better or inferior than other towns in Europe.

Patrick Shaffrey

Introduction

A few years ago some commentators considered that the role of Irish towns and villages was becoming obsolete. Indeed, they went so far as to say that many smaller towns and villages had no economic future and, therefore, should be allowed to die gracefully away — urban euthanasia as it were. There was talk of growth centres—industrial zones—expanding regions — the small town had no place in the planners dream — 'Bigness was beautiful'. Now, however, all the present signs suggest that towns are not dying but are in fact alive and doing very well indeed. They are changing their traditional role from that of a market centre to one with an emphasis on employment or residential activities. This process is resulting in physical change and it is the implications of physical change on towns and on their architectural character that this book is concerned with.

Present trends suggest that expansion will continue for the foreseeable future. Notwithstanding any current lull it seems probable that Irish towns and villages will experience more physical growth over the next twenty-five years than has occurred over the last three hundred. In other words, we are going to build as much again as is already standing to-day.

What are the results going to be like? Will all towns look the same? Can this expansion be directed and co-ordinated in such a way that the essential quality of our towns and villages is not lost forever? Or will those of the future look no different from their British, American, and European counterparts? What do we mean by quality and character? Is there in fact such a thing, and can it be identified and protected?

Our architectural heritage is a vital part of our national culture. It is, with certain regional differences, common to all parts of the country irrespective of cultural and political aspirations. Its protection is, therefore, of the utmost importance. How this generation achieves this will reflect our values as a society. Future generations will judge us on the decisions made to-day.

Furthermore the architectural heritage of Ireland is not just confined to the well known public buildings and certain city streets and squares, it also includes groups of buildings and areas in our towns and villages. These are distinctive by reasons of location, origin, scale, use of materials. In the smaller

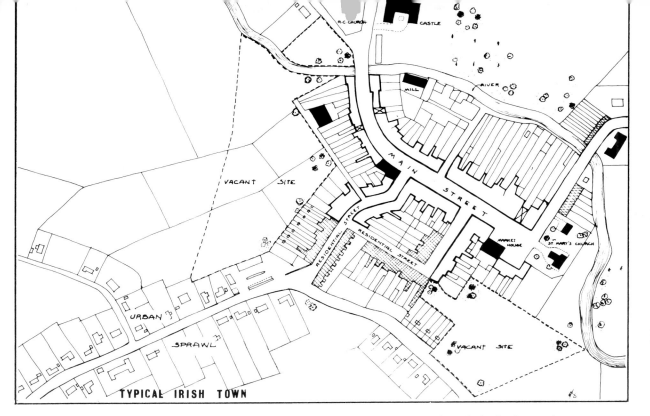

TYPICAL IRISH TOWN

Above - This plan of a typical Irish town illustrates the features to be found all over Ireland; a long main street, two and three storey buildings with living accommodation overhead and shops on to the street. Also to be found are good quality public buildings, long back gardens, charming residential streets close to the centre, vacant sites, and, on the approach roads urban sprawl. The river is practically ignored.

Below - Kells Co Meath a fairly typical example of an Irish town. At first glance places like this may appear dull, but on closer inspection will prove interesting. High quality buildings of various sorts are to be found, and unusual architectural details, but also unfortunately many examples of insensitive modern developments.

village it may be the grouping of small houses with, perhaps, a church, school, river, tree or bridge as the single dominant feature. On the other hand the larger town's character is derived from its layout which, in turn, is influenced by its function as a market or industrial town, or a large provincial centre.

There are many ways in which our architectural heritage can be protected and added to; by restoring and finding a new use for an old mill, by improving in a sensitive and sympathetic manner an existing terrace of houses, by inserting a new building into an existing street, which, although modern in function and design, respects the character and scale of the street. By diverting heavy commercial traffic from a street or small village which is being destroyed by fumes, vibration, and sheer danger to life and limb.

The trouble and unrest in the North of Ireland has resulted in extensive damage to the centres of many towns. Architecturally important buildings and areas have been destroyed or badly damaged. Throughout the Province many areas have been totally and wantonly destroyed, and will require complete rebuilding. There is an opportunity here to ensure that the new developments

We illustrate here several of the ingredients that add to the flavour and character of the Irish Town. Here you will find interesting architectural details, fine shopfronts with good lettering, well designed public buildings and evidence of the use of local materials. All these components combine to give Irish Towns their special charm.

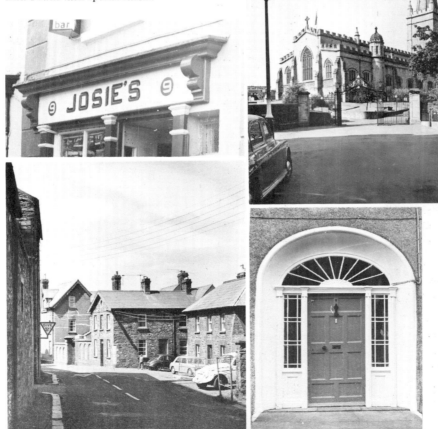

enhance the existing architectural character, and so perhaps some ultimate benefit can be salvaged from this sad and tragic episode.

Our towns cannot be saved from insensitive and needless development, unless the general public has an appreciation of their qualities and an understanding of the pressures on them. It is hoped that this book will contribute towards achieving this objective and at the same time demonstrate how towns can be developed without destroying their character. It is not a plea for preservation, rather the whole emphasis is on physical change which is welcomed, because invariably such changes are the result of social and economic development, without which any society would fade away.

Ireland, both North and South, has a heritage to be proud of in the architecture of its towns and villages. This is under increasing pressures, and will experience economic and social development resulting in physical changes of many types. A common objective for future development should be to make our towns pleasant and safe to live in, to walk about in, to enable all the citizens and visitors alike to enjoy them to their fullest extent, and to hand them on to

Right - Examples of vulgar modern developments for which there seems little necessity, and if allowed to continue could, in a short space of time, erode the quality of our towns.

Below - Northern Ireland - Many fine buildings and pleasant townscapes have been destroyed over the past few years. European history has established a tradition for the restoration of buildings in towns which have been destroyed by wars. Northern Ireland should continue this tradition.

future generations with their intrinsic qualities undiminished.

No two towns are exactly alike, each one reflects its own peculiar history, social traditions, local building materials and craftsmanship. Each has its own architectural expression. All have their particular characteristics which can only be identified after a careful survey and appraisal. Most towns, however, have the same general elements which can form the basis for a better understanding of their qualities. The main theme for the rest of this book will be to demonstrate how towns and villages can be observed and understood by examining their various elements, and identifying the major pressures which are on them. Thus it will be possible for the individual characteristics of each town to be respected and enhanced, and at the same time accommodate new developments.

This need not mean that all new developments should be an exact copy of that existing. Such an approach is both illogical and unnecessary, and a slight on the design ability of the present generation. Modern building must provide for present day uses and functions which are markedly different from those of a hundred years ago. However, standards such as good taste, correct scale, sympathy with surroundings are timeless, and as necessary in this age as in any previous one. Conserving the character of our towns will require imagination and creativity.

A blind conformity to rules and regulations will in the space of a decade or so reduce our towns to mere monuments of uniformity and mediocrity. This is already beginning to happen with disastrous consequences which can be seen throughout the country.

Below - Gort Co Galway - Although the buildings are varied in detail and design, the unity of the street creates an atmosphere and character which is uniquely Irish. Similar examples can be seen in many other towns.

chapter 1

The Nature of
Irish Towns

The settlement pattern in Ireland ranges from isolated houses in the countryside, the ribbon development along the Western Coast to the more complex structures of the larger towns and cities. Ireland is unique in Western Europe in that up to quite recently over 60% of the population lived outside towns or villages of any sort. Although this pattern is changing, the figures from the 1971 census show that about 50% of the population is now living in what is commonly known as the 'countryside'—still a high figure by European standards. In the North of Ireland the balance between urban and rural communities is somewhat different with a bias in favour of urban settlement. It is with the urban settlements that this book is concerned.

Communications and defence have been throughout the ages important factors in determining the location of towns. In the 18th and 19th centuries, the density of population in the Irish countryside was quite high. The major role of the town was to act as a market and service centre for the adjacent country population. The system of communication, mainly horse or foot, influenced the actual location and distance between centres. As a result a pattern has evolved which repeats itself generally throughout the country. The smaller settlements are located from four to seven miles from each other, a distance which could be covered in a few hours on foot. Such settlements varied in population from about 250 up to 2,000. The larger centres from 3,000 to 10,000 population are usually fifteen to thirty miles from each other, and the bigger regional centres of 10,000 and upwards fifty to sixty miles apart. There are, exceptions to this pattern which usually occur with the development of specialist towns, having a less traditional relationship with the countryside.

Many towns, particularly in the South, have evolved on the sites of earlier settlements. This is the reason for the narrow streets and compact form compared with the more spacious Northern towns. Many Northern towns were developed in the 17th and 18th centuries on new sites, free of existing patterns. These were in fact the forerunners of the new towns common in Britain and other countries to-day.

Page 13 - Trim Co Meath

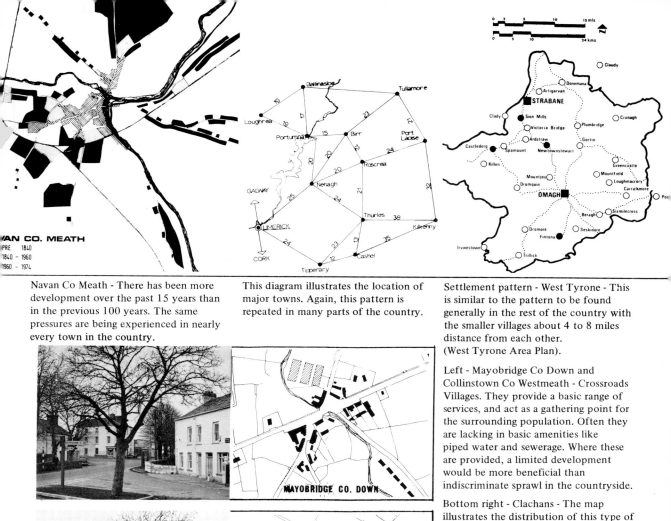

AVAN CO. MEATH

PRE 1840
1840 – 1960
1960 – 1974

Navan Co Meath - There has been more development over the past 15 years than in the previous 100 years. The same pressures are being experienced in nearly every town in the country.

This diagram illustrates the location of major towns. Again, this pattern is repeated in many parts of the country.

Settlement pattern - West Tyrone - This is similar to the pattern to be found generally in the rest of the country with the smaller villages about 4 to 8 miles distance from each other.
(West Tyrone Area Plan).

Left - Mayobridge Co Down and Collinstown Co Westmeath - Crossroads Villages. They provide a basic range of services, and act as a gathering point for the surrounding population. Often they are lacking in basic amenities like piped water and sewerage. Where these are provided, a limited development would be more beneficial than indiscriminate sprawl in the countryside.

Bottom right - Clachans - The map illustrates the distribution of this type of settlement in South Kilkenny.

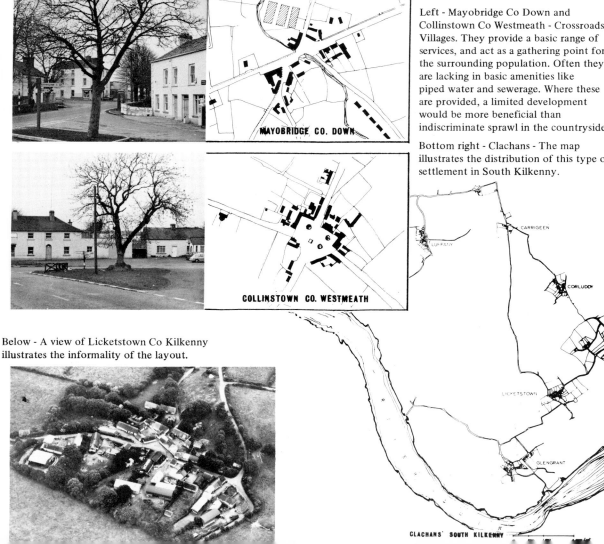

MAYOBRIDGE CO. DOWN

COLLINSTOWN CO. WESTMEATH

Below - A view of Licketstown Co Kilkenny illustrates the informality of the layout.

CLACHANS' SOUTH KILKENNY

The actual physical fabric of towns as we know them to-day was developed in the late 18th and early 19th centuries, from 1840 onwards the amount of rebuilding and development was minimal. Generally our towns never prospered to any great extent. The Industrial Revolution which caused so many environmental problems in other countries did not affect Ireland to any great extent except to a limited degree in the North. Some towns may have done well, certain families and concerns made money, but the overall picture was of stagnation and decay rather than physical expansion.

In this century the rate of development in both parts of the country was comparatively slow. Up to the end of World War Two the emphasis was on social and political matters. After 1945 there was a certain amount of activity, particularly in the housing field. This to all intents and purposes was the only significant physical expansion in many Irish towns for over a hundred years. It was shortlived and lapsed off in the fifties. The net result was that, up to a few years ago, towns had essentially the same physical form as in the mid 19th century. Their distinctive features were still clearly evident — a clean visual break between town and country, a relatively compact town centre, buildings with impressive facades, and many interesting shop fronts. They had not been affected by urban sprawl. Since 1960, the rate of development has expanded enormously. In many towns, there has been more building in the last fifteen years than over the previous hundred years. Unfortunately in the process the character of towns has suffered badly. This will continue unless there is a fresh and imaginative approach to urban development.

Ireland has a wide variety of towns. These can be grouped into a number of categories, which help towards a better understanding of their particular qualities.

First is the *Crossroads Village.* This is the simplest form of settlement and as a general rule consists of a small group of houses, and one or two shops, with perhaps a school and church. Usually it has developed in a piecemeal fashion around the crossroads due to the existence of a church, shrine or other community building, there is often a lack of any unified form. If there is mature planting in the area it will improve the appearance considerably. It is difficult to visualise this type of settlement expanding to any significance in the future.

The *Clachan* is in this category. This is a farming settlement located particularly along the Western Coast, in South Leinster, and the Mourne Country. It is essentially a cluster of farm dwellings. The clachans are in the tradition of the continental agricultural system where the population live in villages some distance from their holdings. The houses are grouped informally without any sense of plan. The lay-out is influenced by the topography and patterns of land ownership. This type of settlement is now disappearing due to emigration, decay, neglect and changing agricultural and social attitudes. A pity, because it is a physical reminder of a past culture as well as an interesting architectural concept. As they are generally located in areas of great natural beauty such settlements have potential for tourist development, or as holiday homes. Others could form the basis for folk villages and community centres.

Second is the *Agricultural Village.* This provides a more balanced level of services, its primary function being to act as a local centre for the adjacent

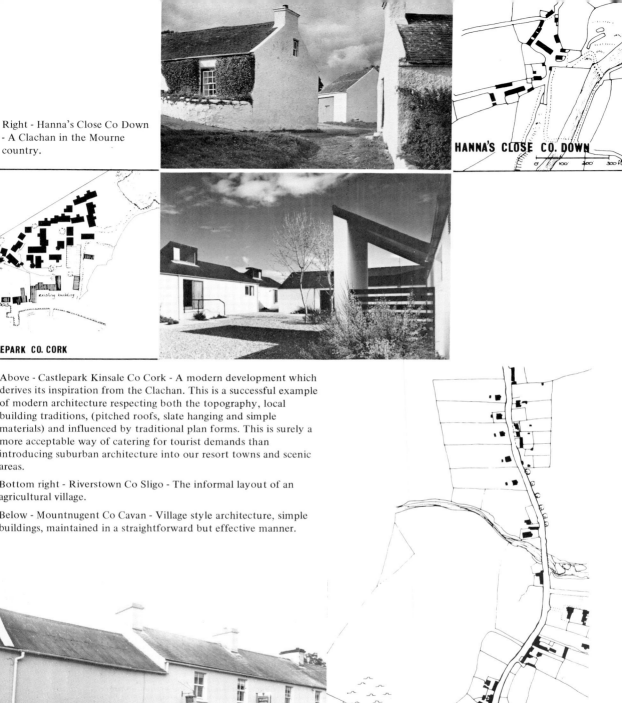

Right - Hanna's Close Co Down - A Clachan in the Mourne country.

HANNA'S CLOSE CO. DOWN

CASTLEPARK CO. CORK

Above - Castlepark Kinsale Co Cork - A modern development which derives its inspiration from the Clachan. This is a successful example of modern architecture respecting both the topography, local building traditions, (pitched roofs, slate hanging and simple materials) and influenced by traditional plan forms. This is surely a more acceptable way of catering for tourist demands than introducing suburban architecture into our resort towns and scenic areas.

Bottom right - Riverstown Co Sligo - The informal layout of an agricultural village.

Below - Mountnugent Co Cavan - Village style architecture, simple buildings, maintained in a straightforward but effective manner.

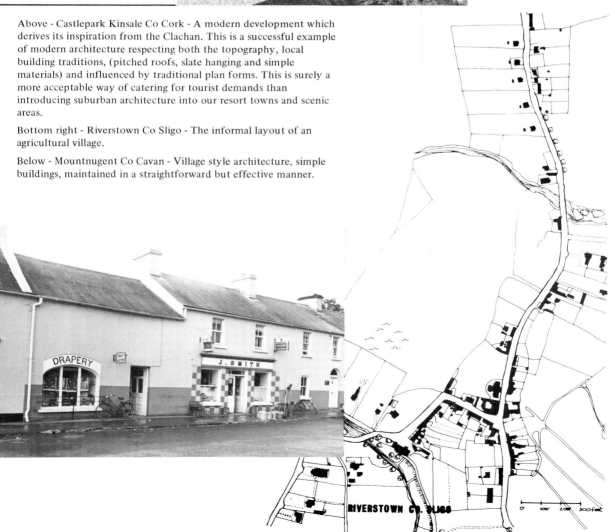

RIVERSTOWN CO. SLIGO

population. There are a few shops, with the usual community facilities such as a church, a school and, occasionally, a local hall. The rest is housing, of simple but attractive design. The overall architectural expression is informal, and small in scale. The buildings are mainly single and two storey, grouped along the road. If there are mature trees this will add dignity, scale and colour to the village. The settlement pattern along the Western Coast is in this category where there are villages with distinctive layouts, influenced by the local topography and patterns of land ownership.

Another type of agricultural village is the *Estate Village*. Its main features are often a pleasant village green or square; attractive housing and public buildings of a high architectural quality. In general these villages will probably develop as commuter or residential villages in association with a larger centre in the same area.

Villages of all kinds are attractive and desirable places to live. They have a definite identity, and can boast of services such as a school, shops, a church, which form the basis of a community—the very items so often absent in the modern housing estate. The design of new developments in villages, however, is of great importance, and should reflect the scale, character and 'genius loci' of the place. The approach to this problem is the same as in other settlements and will be discussed at length in this book.

The third category is the *Market Town*. This is the most common type of settlement in Ireland, both North and South. It ranges from towns with a population as low as 500 to those with a population of 50,000 and over. Market towns are located evenly throughout the country, often at important crossing points on rivers or at road junctions.

The plan form and visual character reflect the function and status of the town. Smaller towns consist usually of a single street, mostly shops with residential accommodation overhead. In some towns there are side streets, mainly residential in character. The shop fronts are of distinctive designs and character. Indeed the shopping streets in Irish towns are an important feature of Irish vernacular architecture, and will be examined in greater detail later on.

The larger towns have a more complex structure with, again, the emphasis on shopping streets. The streets are more varied in appearance and use. There are individual buildings of architectural, historical and social importance. Some towns have areas which as a complete unit are of architectural and townscape significance. The same pattern is repeated generally, shopping and residential being the main uses. It is only in recent years that industry and other commercial uses have developed. The larger cities such as Dublin, Belfast and Cork are even more complex. They now include many smaller settlements which had previously a distinctive character and function, but which have been engulfed by the spread of the cities. Some are now lost beyond trace, both physically and socially, others have the definite physical characteristics of a former separate town and, like Blackrock, Sandymount, and Ringsend in Dublin, the Shankill and Legoniel in Belfast, still exhibit strong social and community traits. Generally, however, such areas could, with thoughtful and sensitive planning, form the basis for local sub-centres within the city region. Visually they are quite distinctive from the general mass of housing which usually surrounds them. There is a mixture of land uses embracing a

CALEDON CO. TYRONE

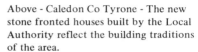

Above - Caledon Co Tyrone - The new stone fronted houses built by the Local Authority reflect the building traditions of the area.

Left - Geashill Co Offaly - Another example of new housing in an estate village, in this case the materials and architectural form are simple — yet effective.

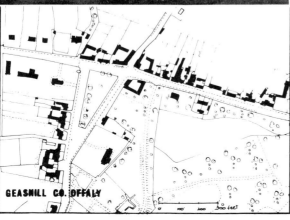

GEASHILL CO. OFFALY

19

concentration of shops, and public buildings.

Fishing Villages. There are numerous examples of fishing villages all around the coast, ranging from a few cottages grouped around a small harbour to the busier fishing ports of Killybegs, Co Donegal, Castletownbere, Co Cork, Kilkeel, Ardglass, Portavogie Co Down and Dunmore East Co Waterford. Over the years fishing villages have had a romantic attraction for many people, and not least artists and writers. There is a vivid and exciting contrast between the gaily painted boats, the solid architecture of the warehouses and the informal and picturesque fishermen's cottages. With improvement to the basic services, in particular water and sewerage, such villages could become extremely attractive places in which to live.

The harbour is usually the important visual element and the layout tends to be informal. Following the rationalisation of the fishing industry many such villages are now declining as fishing centres. Their future prosperity will come from holiday developments, and as locations for second homes. This trend should be positively encouraged, as it will help to alleviate the pressures on the more sensitive areas of the coastline.

Industrial Towns. The dominant visual feature is a complex usually consisting of warehouses, mills and worker's housing. These mills, built of stone or brick, have a robust architectural expression. Many still remain although few are in actual industrial use, and fewer still fulfil their original purpose. As they stand they are a physical reminder of a past technology. However, they have potential for new uses such as flats, hostels, and museums. The shopping or service function of industrial towns is limited and the main emphasis is on industry and housing. Portlaw, Clara and Kilbeggan are examples of industrial towns in the South. There are many examples in the North. Most Northern towns developed considerably in the 19th century, and the whole basis of this new economy was industrial growth, particularly in linen. A classic example is Belfast, which increased in population from 87,000 in the middle of the 19th century to over 350,000 at the end of the century. Bessbrook in Co Armagh is an industrial settlement of particular interest from a planning point of view. Planned on model garden city lines, its development influenced similar experiments in Britain. The development of Bessbrook is described in Gilbert Camlin's book *The Town in Ulster* :-

"The village thus planned was Bessbrook, which was established by Mr John Grubb Richardson in 1846. About that time the Richardson's, a bleaching and warehousing firm, decided to enter the manufacturing end of the business, and Mr Richardson afterwards wrote: "In extending our business, in partnership with my brothers, we were obliged to keep pace with the times and become flax spinners and manufacturers. Hitherto we had merely purchased the brown cloth in the markets to bleach and sell. We had then to decide where we should build linen mills. I had a great aversion to be responsible for a factory population in a large town... so, on looking around, we fixed on a place near Newry.... with water power and a thick population around, and in a country district where flax was cultivated in considerable quantities.... From childhood I was strongly impressed with the duty we owe to God in looking after the welfare of those around us... I had long resolved that we should have a temperance population in our little colony."

Mr Richardson was not primarily concerned with village planning, his interest lay in the temperance movement; but he realized the necessity of providing good homes and the facilities for a full community life for his employees. He was a member of the Society of

Market Towns - Below Bailieboro Co Cavan and
above Limavady Co Derry. These towns are
similar to many hundreds throughout the country.
The classic expressions are the main shopping
streets with residential accommodation overhead.

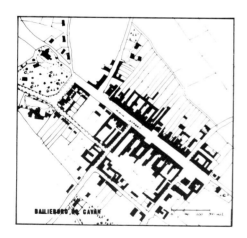

BAILIEBORO, CO CAVAN

Friends and a great admirer of **William Penn**; he, therefore, firmly adhered to the principle that there must be no public house, no pawn shop, and no police in his new village.

The village was planned with a central street, with a square at one end intended as a shopping centre. One side of the square was open and abutting on this was a large green, around three sides of which houses were to be built. Another similar green was planned at the opposite end of the main street; consequently the majority of the houses in the settlement were to be grouped around these two open spaces.

The village had numerous shops, in addition to a general store, butcher's shop and dairy owned by the Company, for the settlement was surrounded by a large area of agricultural land which was in the firm's occupation, so that fresh milk and other produce were readily available. A number of places of worship had been erected and a large open space had been laid out around the lake, where football, cricket, etc., were played. The smallest houses each contained from three to five rooms and the village was lighted by gas supplied by the firm."

Even to-day Bessbrook has no public houses or betting shops. The original settlement is still essentially the same.

Modern industry is more footloose. Nowadays every town and village in the country is seeking an industry of some sort or other. As a general rule, the larger industries tend to go off to the bigger centres and particularly to those centres which have an industrial tradition. There is little doubt that as the economy develops we shall again see the growth of industrial towns. Industry can bring lasting benefits to a town both socially and economically, but can, also, create environmental problems. New industry can in fact help the appearance of a town. The modern factory can and should be a clean and pleasant building, well designed in relation to its function, and suitably integrated with the local landscape. Where this is the case new factories will be an asset to the character of a town. Unfortunately, this is not always so—the appearance of many modern factories leaves a lot to be desired.

Transportation Towns are towns which expanded following the development of the railways and canals and other means of transportation. Dundalk, Portadown, Newry, Cobh, Tullamore are examples. Although the importance of the railways and canals has declined, a tradition for industrial employment helped some of the towns, though not all, to obtain new industries during the current phase of industrialisation.

Military Towns towns have in the past owed their prosperity to the presence of a large military barracks, although often this was combined with the function of a market or transportation town. The barracks may have been established because of the good transportation facilities and the presence of the military helped its commercial prosperity. Many of these towns have now changed their function, the military presence is not as socially or economically important.

Examples are Newbridge Co Kildare, Templemore Co Tipperary, Fermoy Co Cork, Athlone Co Westmeath.

Resort Towns developed mainly in the 19th century due to the growing popularity of holidays. Their growth was aided by improved means of transport, particularly the railways. They are usually located on the coast, but a few inland exceptions are Killarney Co Kerry, Lisdoonvarna Co Clare, Ballinahinch Co Down. The coast was then, as it still remains to-day, a prime attraction for holidays. Resort towns developed on the nucleus of a local

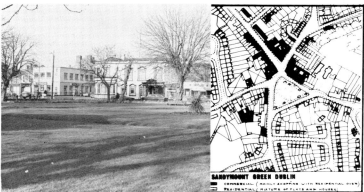

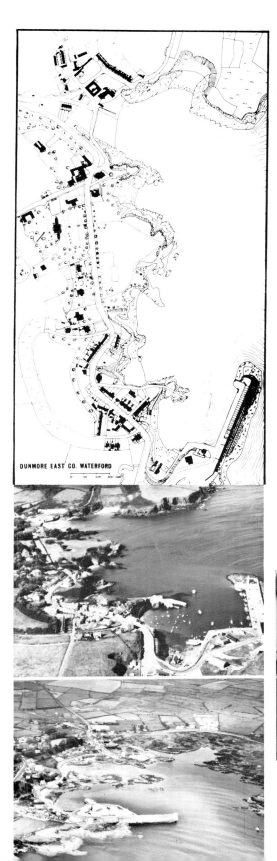

DUNMORE EAST CO. WATERFORD

Above - Sandymount Dublin - A village within a city. The variety of land use emphasises its village characteristics. City planners should recognise the visual and social qualities of communities like this. Many are being destroyed by traffic, and inappropriate land use zoning. The future aim should be to keep these communities as viable entities. Why is it that the new housing areas cannot achieve the charm and character so obvious in places like Sandymount; this is a real challenge to our city planners.

Left - A plan and photo of Dunmore East Co Waterford.

Bottom left - Ardglass Co Down.

Fishing villages - The informal layout is influenced by the topography and gradual development over the years. There are many opportunities for infill development, which should reflect the character of the village.

Below - Coill Dubh Co Kildare - A modern example of an industrial village, which at first glance might look like just another housing estate, but it has an overall coherent form lacking in most modern estates. The high standard of layout, design and maintenance, give this Bord na Mona development a unique character.

bathing place the principal asset of which was a sandy beach, which in turn has become the focal point of the town. Many of these towns have a definite quality and character which varies from the formal terraces of towns like Dun Laoghaire and Portrush, to the smaller scale and more informal groups of houses influenced by the local topography as in Donaghadee, Kinsale and Kilkee. The important visual features are the relationship with the sea and beach, the contrast between the larger and more formal 'stucco' finished Victorian terraces and the smaller houses which have a more romantic appearance. Some resorts are now changing their function and their popularity is on the wane. They are facing increased competition from packaged tour and do-it-yourself holidays. Others however through local enterprise and hard work are continuing to develop.

Commuter Towns are those which are now rapidly expanding because of modern social developments, in particular the tendency for people to travel longer journeys to work and also a reaction against the souless suburbs of the larger cities and towns.

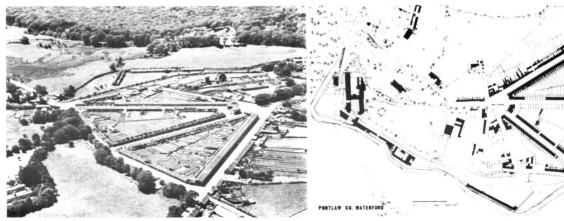

PORTLAW CO. WATERFORD

Above - Portlaw Co Waterford and Bessbrook Co Armagh - 19th century industrial towns which were planned and built as a unit.

Ballynacargy Co Westmeath - The development of inland waterways could mean a new lease of life to this canal village.

Below - Templemore Co Tipperary — A military town with its formal layout superimposed on the flat landscape.

royal canal

BALLYNACARGY CO. WESTMEATH

Many of the smaller towns and villages within easy reach of Dublin, Belfast, Cork and other larger cities are now subject to extreme pressures. They are becoming 'commuter towns' where the main emphasis is on residential development and where it is possible for a village or town to expand fourfold over a very short period. Among such towns are Blarney Co Cork, Oranmore Co Galway, Hillsborough and Groomsport Co Down, Maynooth, Kill and Johnstown Co Kildare, and Swords Co Dublin. This kind of expansion however creates major social and psychological problems in addition to architectural difficulties. On the other hand existing settlements have potential in providing for a better population distribution within rapidly expanding regions. Their development will ease pressure for indiscriminate building in the countryside. They have the nucleus of a community with small but essential facilities, shops, churches, schools, halls. They also have a well defined visual identity. The objective in such situations should be to minimise the psychological problems and ensure that the physical expansion of such villages and towns respects the existing architectural character.

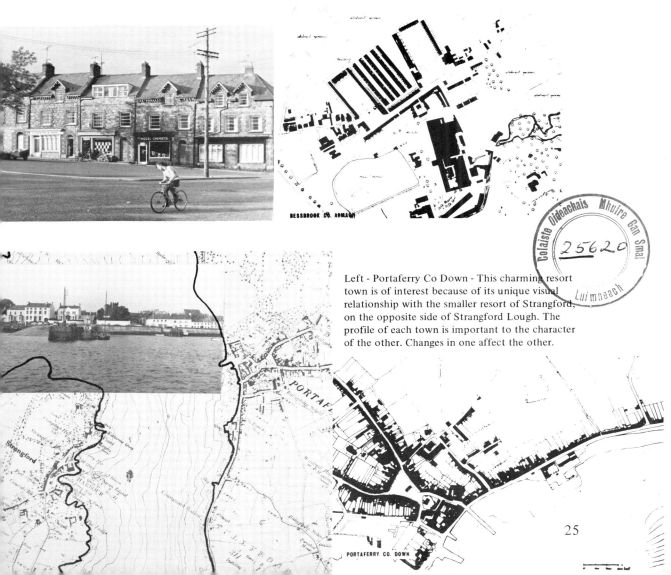

BESSBROOK CO. ARMAGH

Left - Portaferry Co Down - This charming resort town is of interest because of its unique visual relationship with the smaller resort of Strangford, on the opposite side of Strangford Lough. The profile of each town is important to the character of the other. Changes in one affect the other.

PORTAFERRY CO. DOWN

Coláiste Oideachais Mhuire Gan Smal Luimneach 25620

25

KILKEE CO. CLARE

Above - Kilkee Co Clare - A resort town, with an interesting plan, which follows the line of the bay.

Right - Hillsborough Co Down – Architecturally one of the most important towns in the country. Its 18th century central core is almost completely intact. This is due to lack of pressures over the years combined with strong development control. In recent years it has developed as a commuter village to Belfast.

Right - Maynooth Co Kildare – Maynooth is now developing both as a university town and commuter centre. The central area has charm and individuality, but it is being destroyed by heavy through traffic. It needs a by-pass quickly. The University is also developing rapidly but to date this has been away from the town centre. The future holds exciting possibilities for Maynooth. If the by-pass materialises, and the university were to develop east of the town centre, the main street could then become the focal point of the campus with shops, hostels and various facilities.

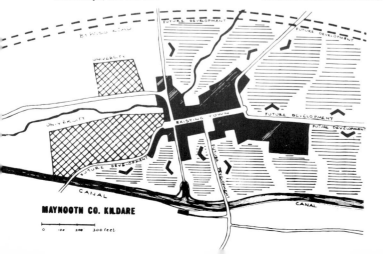

MAYNOOTH CO. KILDARE

0   100   200   300 FEET

Here is an opportunity for Maynooth to become a true University Town in the best European tradition, where town and university are part of one physical unit. This emphasises the need for a creative approach to land use planning.

THE CITTIE OF LIMERICK

Abbey

Chappell

St Cathedrall Churche

Queenes Castell

Thomond gate

y water gate

y keye

A Mill

C Mill

Thomond Bridge

The Shape of Towns

PLAN FORM

The *Plan Form* holds the key to understanding the elements and essential character of our towns and villages. The form will of course differ from place to place and will reflect the local topographical conditions. This plan may vary from a single main street in the smaller settlements to the more complex patterns of the larger towns and cities. Its physical expression may be a central space with buildings grouped around it and with radiating side streets, as in Cahir Co Tipperary, Castlepollard Co Westmeath or Castlewellan Co Down, It may have a closely knit structure influenced by gradual developments over many centuries, and examples such as Waterford, Armagh, Downpatrick, Wexford or Ennis spring to mind. It may on the other hand be a linear type settlement such as Cookstown Co Tyrone, Portarlington Co Laois , or have a single wide street common to many of the smaller market towns such as Beragh Co Tyrone, or Balla Co Mayo.

   At the other extreme are the settlements scattered along the western seaboard where there is an absence of any sort of formal plan. The plan form of a town is not immediately observable to the motorist or to the casual observer, it is something which unfolds as one moves around the town, preferably on foot. The complexities and delights of a town can then be enjoyed to the full—the subtle curves and setbacks which please the eye, and create an atmosphere full of drama and surprise—the back areas rarely seen have their own charm and character, and sometimes offer a glimpse of the countryside from between the buildings. Sadly nowadays this is becoming more difficult, particularly in the larger towns and cities because of the growing traffic congestion.

   The plan of a town is the relationship of buildings, streets and spaces to each other, the relationship with the surrounding landscape whether it be mountains, rivers, the sea, or just small fields. It is something which will generally have evolved over a long period. A full understanding of the plan will bring to light and underline the quality and character of a town and also help us to understand what makes it different from other places. This will mean identifying the important areas and streets, the buildings of interest, the vistas and townscapes, the views out to the surrounding landscape from the town, and, on the other hand, the profile of the town as it can be seen from the various approach roads.

The first glimpse of many towns in Ireland is often the spires of the churches outlined against the sky. To the local inhabitant this is a sign of home, to the traveller a sign that he is near his destination, or just perhaps another landmark on his journey. This particular view is common to most of the settlements in the country and it is one which should not be disturbed. This feature can be destroyed by high buildings in the town centre, equally it can be destroyed by a rash of urban sprawl and developments of all sorts on the approach roads which will blur any distinction between town and country. As the town centre is approached a bend in the street or a slight curve will heighten the interest and add to the character of the town. Such natural lines should be retained. New development should respect rather than destroy them, as happens too often. The bend in the road will help to slow traffic down, a logical and sensible step. Unfortunately some local authorities seem to be determined to straighten all roads irrespective of location.

Town centres are emphasised in a number of subtle ways, by a widening of streets, by the formation of a small square or crescent. This may be accompanied by an increase in size and scale of the buildings from two to three or four storeys or by the location of important community or public buildings at strategic points. Corner buildings and buildings at the end of streets may be architecturally rather ordinary, but because of their location are a crucial element in the plan of the town.

Views out from the central areas will also add interest and excitement. These views may be on to a pleasant courtyard at the back of the street, or more dramatically a view over the surrounding countryside, to adjacent mountains or sea. There are also physical and natural elements which determine a town's character and in many cases will be a major element in its plan. The plan may also be influenced by local topographical conditions as, for example, Inistioge Co Kilkenny, and Kinsale Co Cork. These two towns in particular have much of the same atmosphere and character as European hill towns.

In many towns the river is an important feature of its plan but one which is often largely ignored. Where it has developed as an integral part of the town it adds an extra dimension of quality. Riversides in Athlone, Limerick, Coleraine, Westport, and many other places come to mind. The riversides here can be contrasted with the more numerous examples of the town turning its back on the river.

In coastal towns the relationship with the sea and harbour is important, as in Cobh Co Cork, and Warrenpoint Co Down. The plan form is of significance and can be of considerable assistance in determining an overall concept for any new development area. The town which has a square or crescent for example could repeat this feature in any new development. On the other hand a town with a strongly marked linear pattern suggests that the new expansion also has a linear form, perhaps parallel to the existing one.

Some major element of overall form should be built in at the beginning. If this is derived from or can reflect the existing character of the town so much the better. Often however town expansion schemes are just amorphous housing

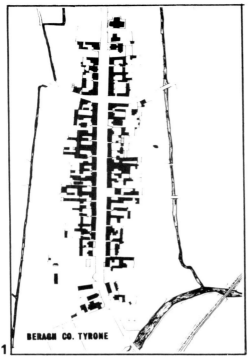

1

BERAGH CO. TYRONE

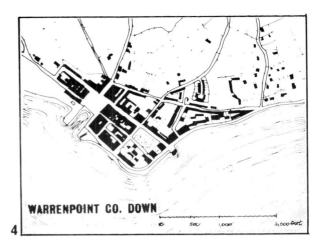

4

WARRENPOINT CO. DOWN

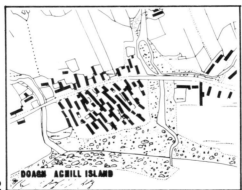

2

DOAGH ACHILL ISLAND

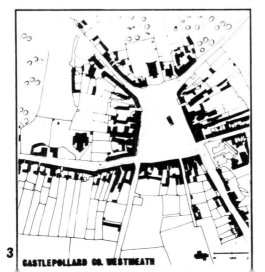

3

CASTLEPOLLARD CO. WESTMEATH

Plan forms of various Irish towns.

1. Beragh Co Tyrone - Typical plan of the smaller town, with a single wide main street which in bygone days, facilitated the holding of fairs and markets.

2. Doagh Achill Island Co Mayo - Highly informal layout to be found in the settlements along the western coast. Although covering a wide area, in a highly dispersed manner, the uniformity of building materials and architectural forms give it a definite character. The densities are quite high. This type of layout could be a more suitable prototype for holiday villages than the 'six houses to the acre' approach often suggested.

3. Castlepollard Co Westmeath - Central square with radiating side streets.

4. Warrenpoint Co Down - In coastal towns the relationship with the sea is usually interesting and dramatic.

5. Armagh City - The original medieval layout has influenced its shape and development over the century. In the older part the streets take the easy and natural way around the hills.

6. Ennis Co Clare - The narrow streets and laneways give the old town an exciting atmosphere.

7. Cookstown Co Tyrone - A linear town with a rigid layout superimposed on the landscape.

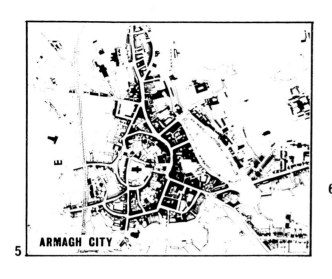

5 ARMAGH CITY

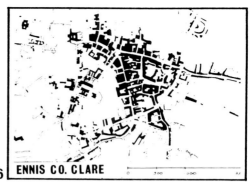

6 ENNIS CO. CLARE

7

7 COOKSTOWN CO. TYRONE

estates which could happen in any town, and for that matter in any country. Decisions regarding the form of future expansion are extremely important because they will determine the character of a town for many years to come.

At present it would seem that provision of services and the ability to acquire land by agreement is the sole criteria and little or no attention is given to design and aesthetic considerations.

The existing physical form of our cities and towns also developed rapidly over a short period. Previous generations by their concern for aesthetic matters have left us a worthwhile heritage. In the current phase of expansion this generation should endeavour to do the same. Town expansion to-day is a difficult and complex problem requiring a great range of skills both technical and administrative. It also can give rise to controversy and debate. What we lack, particularly in the South, are better administrative procedures and legislation. *The New Towns Act (Northern Ireland) 1965* provides an administrative framework for major schemes which reduces speculation and gives local development corporations quite strong powers in acquiring and allocating land. The aim is to gain maximum advantage for the community both from a social and aesthetic point of view. Craigavon New Town, Antrim and Ballymena are all being developed under this legislation.

The Kenny Report on "The Price of Building Land" published in 1973 if adopted and implemented will be of considerable help in formulating long term structural plans which can have an aesthetic merit. It should enable local planning authorities to plan in a positive way and designate land for community facilities or industry. At present such matters are dictated solely by market forces, by the willingness or reluctance of owners to sell. This system often results in the wrong land being developed with the wrong use and at the least appropriate time.

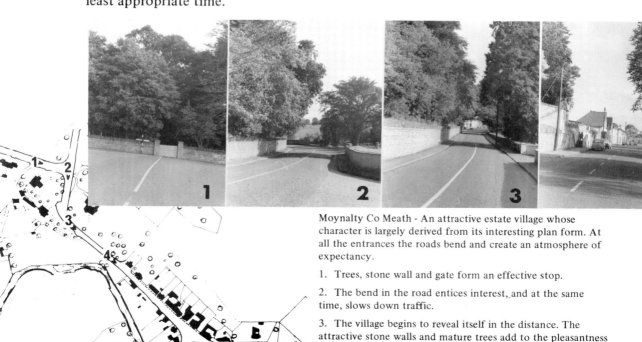

MOYNALTY CO. MEATH

Moynalty Co Meath - An attractive estate village whose character is largely derived from its interesting plan form. At all the entrances the roads bend and create an atmosphere of expectancy.

1. Trees, stone wall and gate form an effective stop.

2. The bend in the road entices interest, and at the same time, slows down traffic.

3. The village begins to reveal itself in the distance. The attractive stone walls and mature trees add to the pleasantness of the scene.

4. The character of the village is at last revealed. Many other villages in the country have similar entrances. They are as much a part of the village character as the buildings.

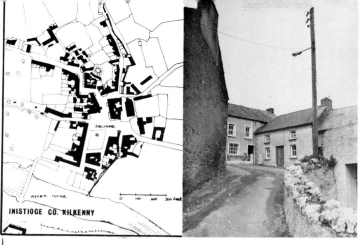

INISTIOGE CO. KILKENNY

Towns like Inistioge have developed gradually over many years, and will present many opportunities for infill development. It is important that new developments respect the existing architectural character and layout. A modern suburban bungalow is not always the most appropriate way.

DUNMANWAY CO. CORK

Left - Dunmanway Co Cork - The relationship between different spaces make the plan of this town interesting.

1. The Fair Green - A triangular space with mainly residential buildings around it.

2. The street narrows at the bridge and this highlights the importance of the market square further on.

3. The river effectively divides the town, and, as is quite common, the potential of the river is ignored.

4. The Market Square begins to open up, and the scale, proportion and atmosphere of this space can be appreciated.

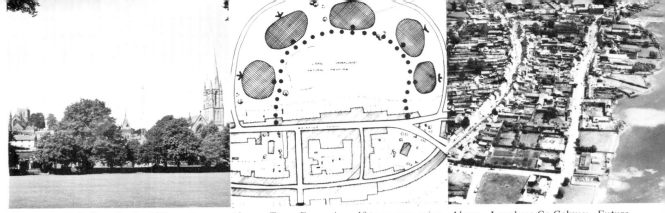

Above - Armagh City - In the 18th century the city developed around the Mall, and now Armagh is fortunate to have this fine open space in the centre. The contrast between the trees, the georgian terraces, the Cathedrals is now one of the characteristics of Armagh.

The present generation are now enjoying the advantages of an 18th century 'land use decision.' (See also page 50)

Above - Town Expansion - If town expansion is considered as a creative process then an overall concept of how the town will look in the future is necessary.

Instead of sprawling out indiscriminantly a town could expand around a nearby lake or park. Such natural features would then perhaps become the dominant visual element in the town.

Above - Loughrea Co Galway - Future development of this town should aim at maximising the potential of the nearby lake.

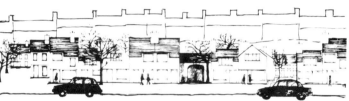

Killeshandra Co Cavan - A small but expanding industrial town. Its principal features are extensive areas of fine parklands, particularly to the east. Located on the brow of a typical Cavan drumlin it has a single main street curving at both ends.

The growth of heavy industrial traffic has created the need for a relief road, and this provides exciting opportunities for the town. It may be possible to build a new street, with shops and houses reflecting the traditions of the old street, but also facing out onto a future town park. Here is an example of how the need for a new road can be utilized to create something worthwhile.

Expansion - It may often be possible to expand a linear town in depth rather than continue in the existing pattern. (See page 45.)

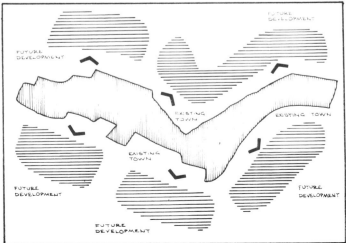

Dungannon Co Tyrone - Profile of an Irish town. The varied patterns of roofs are all dark in tone, and only the church spires break the skyline.

THE PROFILE OF TOWNS

The *Profile* of an Irish town is horizontal, small in scale, with only the churches breaking the skyline. This image is heightened by the general use of pitched roofs of various shapes and sizes and by the even texture and colour of the slates, the commonest form of roofing material. This effect is emphasised when the town is located in a valley or on a hillside. Then the profile, which can usually be seen from a number of vantage points, is of great importance in determining its overall character and visual appearance. There are many towns in the country where the profile of the town is clearly outlined from certain vantage points—Trim, Roscrea and Derry City are striking examples. In such towns any major physical change should be assessed as to its effect on the existing skyline of the town. Ill-considered changes in this regard could be impossible to rectify.

The problem of profile raises the difficult and controversial question of high buildings. To some people high buildings are an expression of modern society and a demonstration of the new technologies which we now have. Any city or large sized town must have at least two or three high buildings to demonstrate its vitality and economic strength. In other words a physical expression of "keeping up with the Jones". The construction of high buildings has of course been made easier by modern building methods, and by the widespread use of the lift. In addition the cost of building land in the city centres has made high buildings more economical. However this is but one aspect of the problem. There is the aesthetic side which is causing controversy and public debate in many cities and towns in Europe, particularly in towns which have central areas of high architectural quality.

A high building is one which is significantly higher than the general height of the development around it. It is a relative term, a five or six storey building in a small town will have more visual impact than an eight or ten storey building in a larger city. By its very nature a high building will stand out and exert a visual influence, perhaps out of all proportion to its actual importance or use. It becomes a major element in the town, and therefore the location of a high building must be chosen with very great care, and the detailed design and materials used are of tremendous importance. There is no room at all for mistakes or miscalculations here as there may be when a new building is constructed within the framework of the existing buildings.

High buildings are generally of two types, the slab block and the tower. The slab block is the most economical to construct. Its scale however is usually overpowering and can create 'a solid wall effect'. The tower block is slimmer in proportion, and as a general rule more expensive to construct, but visually it can be less offensive. The skyline of many towns could be drastically affected by insensitive high buildings. Fortunately there seems to be yet little demand for high buildings in the typical Irish town. But this problem may come, especially in the larger towns. It is already happening in the cities, Dublin is not a particularly happy example of what high buildings can do to a city.

Invariably in debates regarding the merits of high buildings the remark can be heard that—it is a good example of architecture but too high. This remark was made many times regarding the controversial Central Bank Building in Dublin. This argument to my mind misses the whole point of what good architecture within a town is all about. The scale, materials and general form of adjacent buildings should be respected. The new developments should adhere to the general building lines and forms of the particular area in which they are located and should respect the profile of the town. If these elements are missing then a building can hardly be described as good architecture.

A town of any significant size should have a detailed and clearly expressed policy regarding high buildings. Developers, their professional advisors, local associations and the general public should be fully aware of it. This policy should be particularly concerned about the architecturally important areas, where high buildings can do irreparable damage. High buildings in themselves are not necessarily bad, if suitably located, and with good intelligent design they can be a positive element in city structure. For example, they might be located at the entrances and edges of the town where they could be used as a positive design element and not in competition to other existing buildings. They might also be located in centres of the new development areas where they could be conceived as part of an overall design concept and give to such centres a definite visual identity, which could be of psychological importance to the new residents.

Derry City - A distinctive skyline which could be destroyed by indiscriminate high building. This skyline should be respected during the rebuilding of the city centre.

Opposite page - A plan of Derry showing the original walled city.

The Dublin skyline is predominantly horizontal, with only the spires and domes breaking the pattern. In this it reflects the typical Irish town, although on a much larger scale.

The Central Bank building (left) disrupted this skyline. It is not a question of the roof profile, which, if completed in copper, would reflect the other elements in the skyline. A lower building with the same roof profile would have been more acceptable. The adjacent buildings will obviously be developed in the near future. The need to keep the line of the Quays suggests that this development should have a horizontal emphasis with predominantly low rise buildings. Hence the significance of the Central Bank, which may now dominate the profile of the city for generations.

Below left - Bank of Ireland Baggot Street Dublin - This building emphasises that planning cannot be administered merely by rules and regulations. Its expression is modern with a restraint in the use of materials. The scale and proportion of the individual elements reflect the Dublin architecture, but its height and bulk are not at ease with the surrounding area. If the height had been limited to 4 to 5 stories, its impact would have been less disruptive.

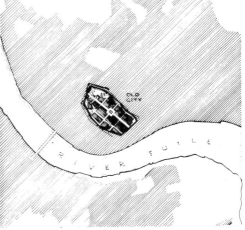

DERRY CITY

PROFILE OF DERRY CITY

Dun Laoghaire - The formal Victorial terraces with a horizontal emphasis, contrast with the church spires, and the extensive landscaping which follows the undulating pattern of the ground, and all enveloped by the Dublin mountains. This particular view is from the East pier - the sheds in the picture are badly situated.

Ballyconnell Co Cavan - A church spire outlined against the sky helps to identify a town in relation to the surrounding landscape.

Belfast - This high building is rather inappropriately located in the old part of the city.

Below - Trim Co Meath - Trim's unique skyline is probably under less pressure than Derry's, but suburban sprawl could destroy its impact.

chapter 3

Entrances

The *Entrance* to any town is an important element in its physical structure. This is true whether the town is approached by foot, private car, or public transport. For many reasons present expansion is mostly taking place at the entrances, particularly on the main roads, and spreading out in an extremely haphazard manner for some considerable distance. This type of development, commonly known as urban sprawl, consists of all sorts of uses and building types, houses, garages, motels, hotels, factories, with an inevitable hotch potch of architectural expressions, and with many buildings and sites left in an unfinished state for years. The overall visual feeling is of chaos rather than order, and all is invariably embellished by a kaleidoscope of poles and overhead wires. Indeed many entrances to otherwise attractive towns are becoming mere 'shanty towns'.

Urban sprawl, however, is not peculiar to Ireland and it is also happening in most other countries. In Ireland we have so far escaped the worst excesses, principally because economic and social development began later. There is therefore an advantage, which if now properly handled could result in a more satisfactory urban/rural relationship for the future. In addition, there is now more public concern about the environment generally. There are also stronger planning laws, although, as will be discussed later in the book, mere laws alone will not guarantee pleasant and attractive towns. Common sense also suggests that we should learn from the mistakes of other countries, but unfortunately the initial results of economic development do not suggest that we are profiting in any way from our situation. Nearly every large town in the country is experiencing urban sprawl in some form or another.

The visual distinction between town and country which was a feature of many Irish towns up to quite recently is now lost in many cases. A definite physical break between what can be obviously distinguished as town and country is generally accepted as good planning, particularly from an aesthetic view point. This of course does not mean that towns should be prevented from physically expanding or that densities within the built up areas should be increased to an unacceptable level.

Page 39 - Kells Co Meath - This pleasant town entrance is
helped by the retention of the hedges and trees.

GREY ABBEY CO. DOWN

Greyabbey Co Down.

1. The approach to the village. The bend creates an air of expectation and at the same time helps to slow the traffic down.

2. On reaching the bend excitement mounts. The stone wall, ivy covered gable and the attractive school house creates a pleasant composition.

3. The character of the village is revealed. The buildings, although of varying design, have an attractive uniformity.

4. More of the village is revealed.

5. The character and layout of the main street is the climax.

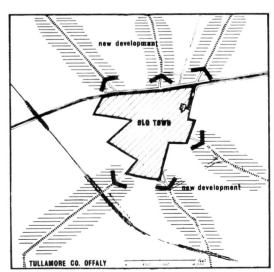

In recent years Tullamore has expanded indiscriminately along all the approach roads.

41

This relationship between town and country has a philosophical and social basis. A town is a place where activities of a social and commercial nature take place and where buildings are the dominant physical feature. In the countryside however, agriculture and its ancillary functions are the primary activity, and nature should be the dominant physical element. In the past these two contrasting activities existed side by side and at ease with each other. We should endeavour to continue this for the future.

Urban sprawl, as well as possessing the obvious visual disadvantages is very wasteful with land. It is common to see frontage development only, leaving hidden behind areas that can no longer be usefully or successfully developed. In addition, the problems for agriculture become more difficult, particularly adjacent to the larger towns. More and more frequently farmers are discovering that it is virtually impossible to carry out the ordinary type of farming activity in a satisfactory way, if close to a housing development. There are problems of trespass, damage from dogs, and generally the people from the new housing estate may have little understanding or appreciation of farming activities. In this regard, however, these intrusions may turn out to be a blessing in disguise.

Up to recently it was generally accepted that any farmer would be prepared to sell his land for building purposes no matter how successfully it was farmed, or how deep his emotional attachment to it. But as agriculture becomes more important in the economic life of the country, and as a result farming land becomes more valuable there may be less inclination by farmers to sell out indiscriminately for urban development. Before long the value of land for agricultural purposes may be a determining factor as to whether it should be used for building or not. This is the case at present in Britain and Northern Ireland where the Ministries responsible for planning consult the various agricultural interests before there is any large scale re-zoning of agricultural land for urban development.

Land after all is a primary natural resource. It is not increasing and we cannot create any more. In Ireland agriculture is the most important use of land and vital to our economy and way of life. Commonsense and prudent management suggest that we balance more carefully in the future the often conflicting needs of agriculture and urban development. Ribbon development is wasteful, and does not make the best use of existing services. In addition it creates a demand for additional services which are expensive to provide. This is particularly true of services such as water, sewerage, public lighting. lighting.

There is in Ireland a tradition of building houses along existing roads, and there still seems to be a desire on the part of many people to locate their house along the most important and busiest road possible. This may stem from a deep rooted feeling to get away from the back areas or remote townlands—getting away from 'the back of beyond'. Roads, and the activities along them, have also been an important part of Irish life for many generations. In the past, although busy, they were relatively safe, and in an age of little communication there would be always something happening along them.

Nowadays many roads are busy, dangerous and noisy. They are a hazard to children and adults alike. The adjacent buildings are subjected to much greater vibrations and pressure than buildings in other areas. With the increase

Top left - Ramelton Co Donegal - A simple but effective entrance. An informal group of houses and a hump backed bridge.

Above - Toomevara Co Tipperary - The picnic area makes an attractive entrance to this village. It stands out as a pleasant contrast to many other towns in the Dublin/Limerick road.

Left - Swinford Co Mayo - The railway arch forms a most exciting entrance. This is not an appropriate location for advertising signs.

Left - Naas Co Kildare

Below - Portlaoise

Entrances typical of many towns in Ireland. There is an air of confusion rather than order.

in road traffic of all kinds, and in particular in the number of heavy transport vehicles, roads are going to be even busier in the future. This heavy traffic will tend to concentrate at the approaches to towns which after all are the origin and destination of most forms of traffic. There are now strong arguments for saying that major roads are the very last place to locate a dwelling rather than to be the first choice. On these grounds alone the *circular issued by the Minister for Local Government in November 1973 regarding residential development was somewhat unfortunate and could in fact lead to more problems than it intends to solve. The reasons for it may be understandable, planning was in certain instances becoming unduly bureaucratic and unnecessarily restrictive. There is also a demand for housing, and a tradition of living in the countryside. This however must be reconciled with the need to conserve the countryside, to ensure that houses are located in safe situations, and that there are certain standards of design and good taste. There need not be a conflict between these two objectives.

There are also legal and administrative causes which lead to ribbon development and urban sprawl. Primarily there is the difficulty in acquiring sites within existing towns, notwithstanding the fact that within the older centres there are many obsolete buildings and areas. Owners are slow to sell sites even though they have not been used in any economical fashion for generations past. Local planning authorities have power to acquire such lands for development. *The Planning and Development Act 1963* and *The Planning Order 1972 (Northern Ireland)* specifically made provisions for the development of such sites and established legislation for compulsory acquisition when necessary. However, compulsory purchase procedure in Ireland is administratively and technically time consuming. In addition it can cause friction at local level. Because of this there is a reluctance on the part of local authorities to adopt such procedures. It is easier for them to acquire land on the outskirts for their own development, and also more difficult to refuse permission, when they cannot indicate to intending developers that there are alternative sites readily available which would be more suitable. There is therefore an urgent need for the compulsory purchase procedures to be updated and improved.

At present it is estimated that it takes up to five years from the making of the compulsory purchase order to the beginning of actual developments on site, that is if confirmed by the Minister. There are a number of preliminary procedures, public inquiries, arguments about the relative merit of the proposal which usually embrace not an intrinsic objection to the proposal but one used merely to create a better bargaining position when the compensation aspects

*The Minister for Local Government in November 1973 wrote to all Local Planning Authorities expressing concern at the increase in the number of planning appeals. He suggested to them that in his view the only sensible way to deal with the problem was to adopt a far less restrictive approach to planning applications, and he advised all Local Authorities to do so. In August 1974 the Minister again wrote to Planning Authorities emphasising even more strongly the same points made in the earlier circular.

Above - Livestock Mart Trim Co Meath - This mart is similar to many others in the country, but by retaining the existing hedge the building is effectively screened. Perhaps we need a society for the preservation of hedgerows!

Left - Dromara Co Down   This village has merged with the landscape. Man and nature respect each other. The result - an extremely pleasant environment.

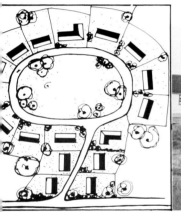

Above left - By developing in depth at right angles to the road and retaining the existing hedges and trees - it should be possible to provide for individual sites with the minimum impact on the landscape.

Above right - Typical residential development to be seen on the outskirts of many towns. Houses are lined along the main road, the hedges are removed; there is no relationship between the houses as regards design or materials.

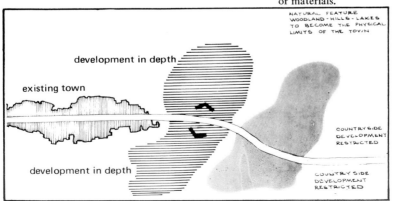

Town Expansion - If town expansion is considered as a creative process than an overall concept of how the town will look in the future is necessary. Existing natural features can provide a distinctive stop to a town's physical expansion.

come to be discussed, and evaluated at a later stage.

It is inevitable however that physical expansion will take place on the edges and on land previously undeveloped. Planning authorities should therefore establish clearly identifiable limits to the towns and villages within their jurisdiction, perhaps to the extent of present developments and then develop in depth the vacant areas. There might also be natural features such as a woodland, lake or hill which would help to define at least one stage of expansion. Such natural features would make an ideal boundary to a town and would add interest and distinction to the particular entrance. The form of expansion will, of course, vary with each particular town depending on the pressures for expansion and the local topographical conditions.

It is also highly desirable for local authorities to acquire, and establish, land banks. Where they have a detailed and well argued plan showing the need for the land required it will invariably be easier for them to acquire it. All building along approach roads however will not cease overnight. In such cases the design aspects of the new development are of crucial importance. With more care in the initial design many problems can be overcome. For example, housing can be grouped at right angles to the road and laid out in the form of a square rather than strung out ribbon like along the main road. This can be carried out and still satisfy the demand for individual homes on their own plots. The same care with design is even more necessary in respect of factories, filling stations and other similar uses. Although there are some examples of well designed factories and filling stations, there are unfortunately too many instances of shoddy building and bad design. Usually the first thing developers do is to bulldoze away all the existing hedges and trees, when in many cases it is quite possible and feasible to carry out development and retain the existing landscape features.

The problem of town expansion is a major conservation problem and needs to be tackled in a fundamental and imaginative manner. It will require changes in administrative and legal procedures, necessitate more controls in the price of building land, and demand more imaginative land use planning and detail design.

On this last point it should be remembered that the most interesting parts of towns are often those built on difficult sites, particularly hillsides. These are the very areas which we may now be seeking to preserve. Unfortunately the general tendency to-day is to develop in as far as possible on flat ground, notwithstanding our greater technology. We should not be afraid to build on steep slopes. Undoubtedly it requires great care and skill, but by respecting the existing landscape we could build new and exciting urban areas. Otherwise towns and villages will continue to expand in an unco-ordinated fashion in response only to market forces and the desires of speculators. Any concern for the common good, an appreciation of the landscape, a respect for the countryside, will be brushed aside. Instead of learning by the mistakes of others we will be copying them. In the more prosperous regions, towns, and villages will be physically linked together by urban sprawl. The whole country could become suburbanised in a matter of a generation or so. This is not the recipe for good planning, and it is certainly not the way to create a worthwhile legacy for future generations.

chapter 4

Central Areas

The central area is the place where the more important activities happen, shops, offices, public buildings are located here. It is the heart of the town, all roads lead to it, all roads have traditionally led to it.

Irish town centres have however a distinctive quality of their own, different from their counterparts in Britain and Europe. They derive their character from the traditional activities of shopping and commerce carried on in a market town, but more particularly from the fact that the physical fabric of Irish towns was built in the late 18th and 19th centuries. This is expressed in the style of architecture and in the layout which was spacious in conception. These are features essentially georgian in character. This influence of georgian town planning can be seen in many towns throughout the country particularly in the North of Ireland.

There are signs in recent years that the dominant role of town centres could be eroded by new developments on the outskirts, in particular new shopping centres. This is a planning problem which requires careful thought. Indeed often shopping developments are being promoted on the outskirts of towns for the very reasons mentioned earlier, i.e. the difficulty in acquiring and intensifying existing land uses within the centres. Local planning authorities will have to measure the true demand for additional shopping facilities generated by rising standards of living, with the need to conserve the centres of their towns, and the traditional trading patterns being carried on in them. They should not wait for a development company to make the first move.

Fortunately the policies adopted by many planning authorities, and the general feeling of local communities is not only to retain the importance of the existing centres, but also to keep their mixture of land uses, and particularly to retain residential areas in town centres. This type of use, above all others, adds character and interest to a town. In many Irish towns the traditional town centre activity is the shop with living accommodation over it. This still largely remains in the smaller towns, but in the larger ones residential uses are being pushed out. The upper floors are used for store rooms, offices, or as often as not left empty. In the larger towns and cities the residential streets close to the town centres are being converted into offices and service areas. Planning

Page 47 - Top - Mullingar Co Westmeath, Bottom - Strabane Co Derry the town centre is destroyed

Land use in an Irish Town.

Top - Rosscarbery Co Cork - A mixture of commercial and residential uses.

Bottom - Cobh Co Cork - Shops with living accommodation overhead like this can be found in the larger towns.

Below - New shopping centres can be visually acceptable but often contribute little to the life of a town. These shopping centres are in effect large department stores which are closed most evenings and on Sundays. Socially they are a poor substitute for the older town centres.

Mountrath Co Laois - The streets converge to form a market square, which up to recently also possessed a market house, this has been replaced by a traffic roundabout. It is important to the character of the square that O'Rourkes is rebuilt along existing lines.

Below - Lisburn Co Antrim - The gentle curve in the street widens into a larger space, emphasising the importance of the market place in Lisburn.

Right - Kilkenny City - To widen streets like this would destroy the atmosphere for ever. It would also contribute little to solving the traffic problem.

LISBURN CO. ANTRIM

authorities have tended to prefer single use zoning for large areas of cities and towns in the belief that this was better planning, and that it was preferable to separate such uses as commercial, residential, and industrial.

This is a legacy from the early days of town and country planning, which was itself a reaction against the physical conditions and urban squalor then prevailing. There is certainly an argument for separating the extremes of the various land uses, for example no one would wish to put a residential development beside a major petro-chemical complex, or provide an open space with a busy road running through the middle of it. But some uses are quite compatible. Shopping, offices, service industry and residential can exist within a single development if the problems of car parking and access are resolved. It is in fact this very mixture of land uses, allied with different styles of architecture, which give old towns their particular feeling and character, and which are attractive to residents and tourists alike.

The recent emphasis by governments and local authorities to increase residential use within the city centres is a positive step and if imaginatively executed could recreate the closely knit communities which were one of the features of city centre life. But it requires an imaginative approach to land use

Limerick and Armagh - In both cities there is a contrast between the formal pattern of the Georgian areas, superimposed on the landscape, and the informal layout of the older parts of the city. Nearly all the early buildings are gone and the physical fabric of both areas date from the same period — the 18th and early 19th centuries. This situation is repeated in many towns throughout the country. New developments within any area should respect and reflect, the existing character and layout.

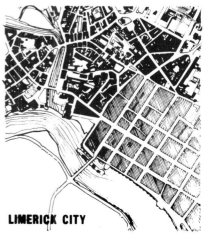

LIMERICK CITY

50

planning and urban design. To demand a certain percentage of residential use in each new development may, in the end, only increase in a mathematical way the amount of housing stock in a city or town centre without at the same time creating a worthwhile environment. The residential element should be considered as an integral part of the development and not provided as an afterthought and mere gesture to the planners.

In certain instances it may be preferable if developers of major commercial and office complexes were required to make a contribution towards the cost of residential development in adjacent areas or that they themselves would carry out residential development in certain selected and agreed locations.

Often towns were developed on the general patterns already established by earlier settlements. In such cases the streets in the central areas generally have a more intricate pattern as the later developments respected the existing laneways and roadways which were usually quite narrow, catering for a slower and different means of transportation. Such a process has given these towns a distinctive appearance, charm and quality which should be retained despite the demands made by modern development.

Left - Mullingar Co Westmeath - The variation in street widths and the curving frontages combine to create a series of different spaces. It is these spaces that give the town centre its character.

Below - Newtownstewart Co Tyrone - A group of attractive houses which lead into the main street. In the West Tyrone Area Plan it has been suggested that this street be redeveloped. Should this happen it is important that the existing street lines be maintained.

MULLINGAR CO. WESTMEATH

The narrowness of the streets, and the small scale of the buildings, create a sense of enclosure excitement and expectation, often missing from the more spacious towns. This type of town exemplified by Wexford, Kilkenny, Kinsale, Ennis, Dromore, Downpatrick, and others are an important part of the Irish Architectural Heritage. The physical form of such towns highlight the conflict between the pressure to provide for increased traffic at all costs and the desire to retain the essential character of the town. The usual approach is to widen the streets either on a wholesale basis or gradually as property is being developed. This certainly is not the answer to the traffic question. Experience in other countries has proved this. Many towns have certain areas medieval in concept and others laid out on georgian principles. Armagh and Limerick are two examples. Sometimes it may only be a matter of a few streets or even groups of buildings contrasting with each other, or it might be the 'old Irish town' and the 'planter's new town'.

Central areas are subjected to pressures of all sorts from increasing commercial requirements, growing traffic problems, and the need to physically renew old and worn out buildings. They are often however for all their problems pleasant to look at, to walk about in, and to live in. To retain these priceless assets and at the same time accommodate necessary change is at the heart of urban conservation.

Birr Co Offaly - Spacious town centre typical of an 18th century planned town.

Ennis Co Clare - The narrow lanes, streets and wider spaces all combine to create a town centre with an exciting atmosphere. When redevelopment takes place it is important that existing street lines are adhered to.

chapter 5

Redevelopment~
The Problem of Infill

The central area of a town by its very nature generates economic activity of all sorts, which in turn creates pressures for physical changes. To cope with these physical pressures in a positive way, and at the same time protecting the intrinsic merits of the town is of course the essence of urban conservation. It is unlikely that town centres and other built up areas will be redeveloped without land changing hands either by agreement or compulsorily acquired by the local authority. As pointed out earlier compulsory purchase is extremely slow and new procedures are necessary. However even with improved administrative procedures redevelopment in towns is a difficult and complex problem, demanding new techniques. The traditional planning approach to redevelopment particularly within the larger towns and cities has been by what is known as "comprehensive redevelopment areas". Large areas were declared obsolete because of the existing physical conditions, and in particular the need to remove slums and unfit dwellings.

According to this approach 'comprehensive redevelopment' has a number of advantages, it provides for a more beneficial use of land, and will result in less conflict between traffic and, for example, residential areas. It is possible to provide better social facilities such as playing fields and parks. Above all it provides an opportunity to create over a wide area an environment related to modern needs. Many master plans have been prepared along these lines for the redevelopment of older areas, especially in Europe and the United States of America. This in theory is a sensible approach indeed, but with the implementation of such plans there have been many difficulties.

In the older residential areas when redevelopment takes place the original residents are often re-housed in the new estates on the fringe of the city. When eventually the houses appear in the old city centre areas they are often allocated to newcomers who have no roots with the community there. As a result there has been a wholesale disruption of close knit communities causing many social problems. Land acquisitions were long and protracted and usually resulted in a watering down of the original concept. Notwithstanding this, local authorities have often felt obliged to refuse permission for redevelopment for fear of compromising the overall concept. This was clearly evident where traffic

Page 53 - Top - An infill site, Middle - a rare example of good infill
Bottom - the more common solution.

Above - This aerial view of Ballaghaderreen Co Roscommon emphasises the amount of open land still to be found in the centre of many towns. There are opportunities here for exciting infill development, which could add to the character of the town, and, of course, cut down on the need for sprawl at the edges.

Left - Three poor examples of modern infill work.

Below - Two good examples of infill, one in a small village and the other in a city street.

planning was concerned.

Comprehensive development plans can therefore cause confusion and give rise to what is commonly known as 'planning blight'. Planning blight is the erosion of the economic and social viability of an area because of a previous decision, which envisages redevelopment at some time in the future, in accordance with a very detailed overall plan. Areas thus affected have the same seedy and dilapidated appearance in every country, shops and houses boarded up, the occupants gone away to other parts of the city, vacant plots of land used as car parks, community buildings under-utilised and rundown and schools and churches closed. A large part of the central areas of cities and the large towns are suffering from these conditions, often due to ill conceived and grandiose traffic plans, vague ideas for comprehensive development, and perhaps most of all, the lack of a positive policy for infill or gradual development.

Public and planners alike are now having second thoughts about such an approach towards redevelopment. It is not however the concept of having a proper environment on a comprehensive basis and suited to modern needs which should be reconsidered, but the means of implementing and achieving such a concept. It is now accepted that to carry out redevelopment on too large a scale can be socially and visually disruptive. It is better to tackle the redevelopment on a gradual basis with more flexible plans, but at the same time with clear cut social, physical and aesthetic objectives. In other words, to create an evolutionary process to urban redevelopment. The end product of any scheme would be an environment that is pleasant safe and aesthetically satisfying, and also at any time during the development the social and environmental conditions are as satisfactory as possible for the people living there. Not that there can ever be an 'end state' as such in cities and towns.

Such an approach is quite appropriate to the typical Irish town. Here due to an absence of extreme pressures, comprehensive redevelopment on a large scale would not be viable anyway, and most developments will take place in an ad hoc manner, over a long period. This should not mean an absence of planning, or that development should take place in an uncoordinated manner.

The most sensitive, and difficult, problem is infill development, particularly in towns with a high architectural and townscape quality. Infill developments can occur in a number of different situations, firstly, the complete renewal of an existing building or group of buildings, secondly, the development of a vacant site or the grounds of a large house now functionally obsolete, thirdly, it may be nothing more than a small development – the improvement to a shop front or the restoration to a group of houses. In all these situations there are constraints involved.

The scale, character, design, and materials used in adjacent buildings are all matters which should influence in some way the architect's and developer's approach. Infill development is a sensitive grafting job, and, like all such operations to be executed with success, requires deep understanding knowledge and appreciation of the parent body. Unfortunately in the case of urban design this rarely happens. Too often developments bear no relation whatsoever to the surrounding buildings and instead of an improvement in the general appearance add such a discordant note as to be destructive to the

Above - Moville Co Donegal - The buildings on the left may have fulfilled their function. There is an opportunity here for redevelopment which should add to the character of the town. The proposed new buildings reflect local architectural traditions.

Above - Ballinasloe Co Galway - An attractive scheme of flats has been built and off street car parking provided in what was previously an under-used back garden.

Below - Wexford Town - It is important that a pitched roof is used, and the vertical proportion of the existing facades continued when this site is being developed.

Above - Gort Co Galway - These buildings are in obvious need of repair. They are an integral part of the street and are worthy of complete restoration.

character of an entire street. Some are so ill at ease with their neighbours as to cause wonder whether the developers or their advisors, if any, visited the site beforehand or were subject to any planning control whatsoever. It is hard to believe in these situations that one of the aims of physical planning is to ensure orderly and proper development of our towns and cities, taking into account their existing architecture and townscape qualities. But to legislate for good design is one thing, to ensure that it is carried out is an extremely difficult matter.

Good infill requires more understanding and perhaps some humility on the part of the developer. It also demands a more detailed appraisal of the intrinsic character of a town or city by the local planning authority for the benefit of the general public, the politicians architects and developers, and others engaged in the rebuilding of towns. This is not an impossible task, it is not unduly expensive, and will not create unnecessary difficulties for any property owner. On the contrary, there are a whole range of benefits both social and economic as well as visual to be gained when infill development is properly carried out. It can add considerably to the appearance of a town, and as well make a significant social and economic contribution to the town's development.

A feature of the land use pattern of Irish towns are the long rectangular sites with only the front being used in any intensive way, the backs usually housing an assortment of outbuildings and sheds. Groups of derelict houses, and vacant sites can also be seen in many parts. In general the use of land in built up areas is not by any means intensive and there are many opportunities to improve the situation. Some back areas have all the signs of being underused for generations. Sometimes there is access from a back road, more often the access is from the front by means of an archway, an attractive feature in many towns. This in itself is a design element of great potential which can be retained to provide an attractive entrance to backland development.

A policy for infill development and redevelopment will also require a more imaginative approach to development control. Planning requirements cannot be equated with the situation pertaining in new development areas. To insist on rigid parking standards, widths of roads, sight lines, densities, plot size within towns may frustrate and inhibit developers rather than stimulate them. Each particular proposal will have its own requirements and constraints and should be assessed on its actual design merits and social objectives. Indeed it may be necessary to relax regulations to preserve certain design and aesthetic qualities. Many of the older and more interesting parts of towns could not be built if they were to conform to current regulations. These are the very areas, which local groups now wish to preserve, and where the tourists and visitors gather.

There seems to be a general approach by many planning authorities in thinking that all the towns in the country are the same and they can all be planned in the same way by conforming to the same set standards. An examination of many plans will reveal a concern—some people would say an obsession, with traffic matters, width of roads, sight lines, parking, even in some instances to laying down regulations for filling stations. This latter point is almost amusing. Since the energy crisis (and even before it) additional filling

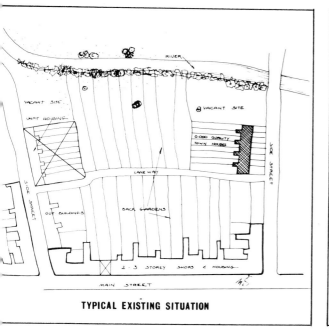

TYPICAL EXISTING SITUATION

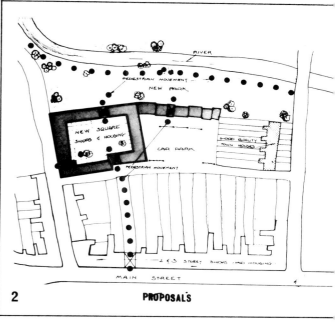

2 **PROPOSALS**

MAIN STREET

The long back gardens found in many towns afford exciting possibilities for infill development. The advantages are many. Derelict areas can be improved, the river opened up, perhaps a new space added which would contribute to the architecture of the town. Housing, shops, car parking and other community facilities can be provided in this way.

4 ENTRANCE TO NEW SQUARE

5 NEW SQUARE

stations are perhaps the least important requirements for any town.

At the same time there was little or practically nothing about the landscape setting, the architectural and townscape quality; the very aspects which give the town its distinctive character. There are no firm proposals to guide future developers as to what might be acceptable. This is of course a negation of what good planning is all about, and if this policy is persisted in, all the towns in the country will eventually look the same.

A more imaginative approach will not necessarily mean going overboard with existing regulations, but in reality tailoring them to the requirements and needs of each particular town. Local planning authorities should therefore prepare guide lines which the general public and their professional advisors can interpret without great difficulty. Each particular town will have its own guide lines depending on its character, and the nature and type of pressures for development. These guide lines should be as informative as possible, the overall philosophy should assist and direct development in a positive manner.

One possible approach will be discussed in detail later in the book but a number of simple points can now be made. Development should respect the general character of the town; the character of many Irish towns comes from the contrasting relationship of dark slated roofs of various shapes and sizes and bright colourful facades. The traditional approach was simplicity and restraint. There was not, of course, the same range of materials as is available today. Stone and plaster were most common, and occasionally, brick. An unrestrained and vulgar use of materials such as imitation brick and stone, plastics and mosaics contribute nothing to the character of a town and, in most instances, only add to the expense of the building. Unfortunately it now appears common practice to use as many different materials as possible on a building.

Existing building heights and building lines should be retained wherever possible. It is the overall consistency of building lines and heights which give unity to our towns even though the detailed architectural expression is quite different. Look at any town, the main street may very well contain a whole variety of buildings of different types and with different functions, but because of the general consistency of building heights and lines such differences are not immediately apparent, and the overall impression is of a complete unit, spacious and full of vitality. But above all the character of the central parts of towns comes from the actual physical attachment of one building to another. This creates unity and coherence in towns, it has done so for a thousand years or more. This character and quality is usually absent in the newer development areas, and sadly and more importantly in the infill development which takes place in the older areas. With modern techniques it should be possible to retain this relationship without compromising standards of privacy and also to provide better standards of access which are a necessity nowadays.

Good infill development does not necessarily imply an exact copy of what was there before or of what the adjacent buildings are like. In many instances new buildings can, and should, reflect contemporary needs and contemporary uses. This was the case in the past where buildings reflected current characteristics, standards and tastes. It is no less important now. It can be done without being unsympathetic to the older architecture. There is indeed room for good modern architecture in any town or village.

chapter 6

Amenity Areas

Open spaces and amenity areas in and around towns can take various forms. They can be designed and made by man, or they can be natural, in a sense a 'gift from God.'

The natural amenities might be rivers, lakes or the sea coast and would also include woodland and open areas and indeed individual trees. The main characteristics of these natural features is their openness which provides a pleasant contrast to the built up areas.

On the other hand, amenity areas may be man-made spaces created by a conscious design decision. The squares and crescents which can be seen in many towns are an example. We find also those areas which in the past had a special function such as a fair green or a market square. These are important elements in the design of a town, because as we have seen, the original purpose of most towns was to act as a service and market centre for the population in the surrounding countryside. This function may now be obsolete or have undergone radical changes.

All these elements add distinctiveness, spaciousness, and character to a town. Some towns may have one or other of these features, which can provide an identity that marks it apart from other towns in the same area. In an era of increasing uniformity all over the world, distinctive features, whether they be architectural, natural or cultural, are tangible assets that local communities should value and cherish dearly. The planning of a town should take such features into account, ensuring that they will play a positive and imaginative role in its physical structure.

In larger towns major expansions should reflect if possible the amenity features which exist in the older parts. For example a town with squares or crescents should continue this concept in the new housing areas. Those which have the good fortune to be located near a major natural feature perhaps a river, lake, or on the sea coast should recognise and utilise such an asset. This need not necessarily preclude all building. Indeed the presence of a natural feature may be a factor in deciding that people should be living as close to it as possible. With imaginative site planning a lake or river could then become the central feature of the town without always being on the periphery.

Left top - Coleraine Co Derry - an accessible river can become a pleasant amenity.

Centre - Athlone Co Westmeath - opening up a river may require nothing more than a simple pathway as in this example. The river provides a pleasant setting for boating and reading.

Bottom - Newtownstewart Co Tyrone - The town ignores the river, a situation to be found all over the country.

Right - River cleaning operations - The Dodder River in Dublin.

Below - Typical of many Irish towns, Boyle Co Roscommon turns its back on the river. There may be opportunities for redevelopment, perhaps providing an amenity area, or new housing with a pleasant outlook. Local Authorities and voluntary groups can give a lead in this kind of work.

Because of expansion and development there will be many opportunities to open up a river for recreational or amenity use; to ensure the renewal of a market place or fair green by improving the existing buildings or by the insertion of new buildings, to make better use of canals and harbours because of the new demand for recreational and leisure activities, to create a more meaningful use for the woodlands and landscaping. These things will not happen by a mere mention in the plan. The planning authority, assisted by the local community associations, should take active steps to stimulate such developments. Each particular case will demand its own individual approach.

RIVERS

A river in itself provides a microcosm of society from its source in the hills where the physical pressures of urbanisation have not yet been felt to any great degree, and where nature still reigns supreme, to its end at the sea where in the cities nature has been superceded by the works of man, sometimes in a pleasant and artistic fashion but, unfortunately too often, in a brash and ugly way. It will have grown from a small brook with crystal clear water to a busy estuary with its waters heavily polluted. On its journey the river passes villages and towns all different in character and function, sometimes utilising the potential of the river but all too often ignoring it.

A river is an important natural feature that adds interest to a town. For historical reasons many towns are located on or near a river. In the past they were sources of power, and means of transportation. A bridging point on a river was always considered an appropriate location for a settlement. Many have grown into major towns. Some are fortunate enough to have the river running through their centre, and therefore it has become an interesting feature in the visual quality of the town. Dublin is an example where the river and quays are architecturally of international significance. Other examples are Cork, Coleraine, Fermoy, Westport and Clonmel. Most towns, however, for historic or other reasons have turned their backs on the river. As a result instead of being a valuable asset to the town, the river becomes a dumping place at best, and at worst an open sewer. Refuse of all kinds can be found in them. Many local societies now spend considerable time and energy trying to clear the mess. In retrospect it now seems a pity that such natural features did not have a design influence as the town evolved.

Towns however are not static items. They are in continual change from year to year, and from generation to generation. Present policies should now utilise these changes and pressures in a positive way by ensuring that natural features will have a more important role in the architectural character of a town. However, although it would not be practicable to turn a town right around and face it on to a river, it should be possible with imaginative planning to open it up both visually and also from an access point of view. The aim should be to make the best use of its amenity potential, and create a new design element in the structure of the town which will last for many generations.

There are sensible arguments for redeveloping buildings close to the river that are of no economic or structural importance. The plans would identify the areas which need redevelopment, and will ensure that

The West Tyrone Area Plan proposes a riverside park for Omagh. This is an exciting possibility which should be implemented.

Above - Donaghadee Co Down - Trees as well as buildings should be cherished, and of course should be the subject of tree preservation orders.

Below left - Oldcastle Co Meath - One single tree can transform an entire scene.

Below right - Malin Co Donegal - This private garden has a Japanese like simplicity, but the colours, materials and character are in the best Donegal traditions, whitewashed walls, slated roofs, reds and browns for doors and gates. Located at the entrance to the village, it is a good example of a private space contributing to public amenity.

when redevelopment does take place access to the river or natural feature will be opened up, and also suggest where recreational and other facilities should be located. It will also be important to establish pedestrian ways along the river perhaps leading out into the open country or on to another open space. There may also be possibilities because of road improvement schemes or housing redevelopment to acquire land in larger pieces, taking into account the environmental possibilities of a nearby river or natural feature.

A river which is open and accessible will be an asset to any town. There will be fewer problems from dumping and neglect, because the river will now become an important feature in the town rather than an open sewer which it may have been for many generations previously.

The same arguments equally apply to lakes, the sea side and other natural features. Traditionally however, there is not the same difficult situation with regard to the coast. As a general rule in coastal towns the buildings face the sea rather than turn their backs on it. Often there are problems of access which can be overcome by positive planning and management. The guiding principles are the provision of proper access, detailed design considerations to any new structure, and specific control of land use. The detailed design in coastal towns is particularly important. Over the years certain traditions have evolved with regard to seaside architecture. It has a vitality and atmosphere of its own. There is a positive use of colour, particularly black and white. Details are simply but sturdily expressed. This simplicity of expression can be found in a small fishing village and in a large holiday resort.

TREES AND PARKLAND

Of all the natural elements that add character and distinction to a town none perhaps is more common than trees. Trees have been important to man from time immemorial. They have been a source of raw material in addition to providing pleasure both aesthetically and emotionally. The latter point is relevant when discussing trees and landscaping in urban areas, whether it is a group of fine mature trees or an individual one in a small suburban garden. A single tree can transform an entire town and give it quality and softness. Trees add variety and colour. They bring nature into the town and reflect the moods of the seasons.

Existing trees should be carefully protected wherever possible. The Local Government and Planning Development Act 1963, and the Planning (Northern Ireland) Order of 1972, both have made specific provision for the preservation of trees. Unfortunately very few tree preservation orders have been made to date. As a result in many towns where the trees are of fundamental importance to its architectural character they can be demolished without any reference to the local planning authority. The only permission needed is from the local police station, and this only in respect of the safety regulations to be followed in the actual felling of the tree.

Imaginative tree planting and landscaping can transform the most ordinary street or housing area into quite a pleasant environment. Sometimes the width of the street is overpowering in relation to the height and scale of the buildings. This happens in the smaller towns where the level of street activity is not great. Here tree planting would add considerably to its character. A comparison

Above - Macroom Co Cork - The photograph was taken around the turn of the last century and part of the estate has been turned into a public park.

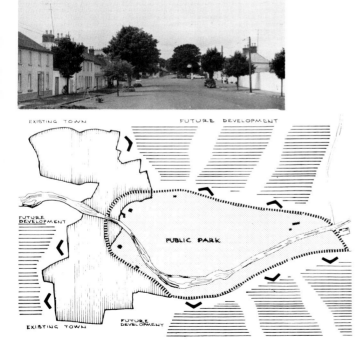

Above - Sixmilecross Co Tyrone - Tree planting can considerably improve the appearance of the wide main street. (From West Tyrone Area Plan).

Left - Clonmellon Co Westmeath - The present generation are enjoying a legacy of tree planting.

Left below - Trim Co Meath - With careful planning there is a possibility of creating a public park along the River Boyne incorporating many historical remains. This area should now be kept free from all development.

between those towns which have inherited a legacy of tree planting with other more austere looking towns will emphasise this point. There are opportunities here for local organisations to remedy this, and many have started planting. Planting however must be carefully protected and maintained, particularly during the early and formative stages. It is always a sad sight to see young trees destroyed by vandalism or dying through lack of care. Whenever this happens the policy should be to plant again and again if necessary.

Existing trees in urban areas are subject to continuous pressures from local authorities and the general public who may not understand the value of proper pruning, maintenance and care. They are often under attack from developers whose only concern is to get the maximum amount of development from any particular site, and from the general wear and tear due to pollution and other hazards usually found in cities and towns.

One of the great effects of the 'Tidy Town's Competition' has been the impetus given to tree planting in the towns and villages throughout the country. The entrances and central areas of many towns have been greatly improved by this. The enthusiasm, concern and hard work of these local committees will be appreciated by future generations.

A feature of certain towns are extensive areas of mature woodlands, formerly the grounds of a large estate. The house itself may be gone or changed beyond all recognition. Here can be found magnificent mature trees of many varieties and with comparatively little effort such estates could be converted into town parks. This has already happened in some towns with obvious social and visual benefits. Even the smaller scale 'house and gardens' formerly belonging to a prosperous merchant, or some local dignitary, has potential for a park and amenity area. These properties when situated in the middle of a town invariably come under pressure for development. There is a strong case to be made for not developing such sites, but retaining them to provide a 'green lung' in the town centre. This is not always possible. In this event the existing landscaping should be integrated into the future development even though this may mean a smaller financial return to the developer.

OPEN SPACES

With the greater emphasis on leisure and recreation many local authorities are concerned with the provision of open space facilities, particularly in the new housing areas. The demand might be for playing-fields, public parks and recreation areas. This need is frequently overlooked. Even when it is provided it is often wrongly located, unimaginatively laid out, and poorly maintained. Many planning appeals by residents' associations relate to the problem of open spaces. Here again the impossibility of relying on rules and regulations only to achieve a pleasant and attractive environment, is all too clear.

Local development plans usually stipulate that new housing areas must have at least 10% of the site as open space. In principle this sounds a laudable aim, but in many cases the actual result on the ground is not at all satisfactory. The 10% may be provided by measuring off a series of bits and pieces of ground left over after the houses are laid out. They are unconnected to other open spaces or to schools, shops, recreational areas. The same comment can be

Above - Swords Co Dublin - There is an opportunity to create a comprehensive open space system in this rapidly expanding town. This would connect the countryside (A) to the old historic part of Swords (B) and continue on towards Malahide (C)

Such an approach would be much better than considering the individual housing estates as entities in themselves, all with their 10% open space.

The trees in the grounds of the large house (D) are important to the character of the main street, and could become a small town park. However, even if it is developed for housing, it is absolutely imperative that the existing trees be retained.

Below - Every large urban area should have a comprehensive open space policy. Ideally they should all be linked together.

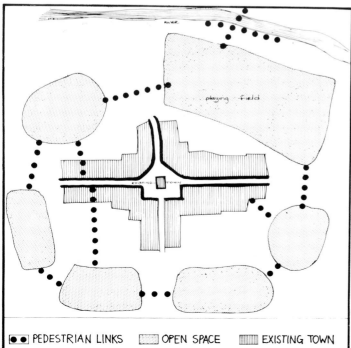

Above - The sketch illustrates the result of bad pruning that occurs too often. Note the profusion of snags where the branches should have been cut back to the fork and the excessive pruning of the leaders. The branch cuts are not painted or otherwise treated against infection and rot.

●● PEDESTRIAN LINKS   OPEN SPACE   EXISTING TOWN

made about landscaping and tree planting which is often considered as a cosmetic, to be added afterwards to satisfy the whim of the local planning officer, or the local residents association. All trees in an area to be developed should be accurately plotted on the submitted plans, listing the types, species, condition and all other necessary information. This information should be provided before the proposals are even considered by the planning authority.

There may be instances where the need for open space is not so great, for example where housing is close to a major amenity feature, a lake, public park, along the coast, or within the town centre. In other places it may be necessary for much larger open spaces considerably above the 10% mandatory requirement, particularly if there is a need to include an existing amenity feature into the open space system. There are no hard and fast rules. Each town and each case will require its own solution. There is however one overriding approach which should be adopted wherever possible, all open spaces should be considered as part of an overall system for each town. Every town or village plan should include a strategy for open spaces. The ultimate aim would be to connect all into a continuous system, where by the nature of things the pedestrian would have precedence over the motor vehicle. The town square, parks, large gardens, public buildings, rivers, open land and the adjacent countryside could, in some way, be joined together. Sometime the links would be very strong and clear cut, at other times more tenuous as for example, parks, playing fields and other open spaces linked together by footpaths or by roads where the traffic is not heavy. Ideally it should be possible to meander from the heart of the coutnryside into the town, or vice versa.

Such a system could not be built up over night. It is a long and gradual process. It may involve the acquisition of land, agreements with property owners, it may also have to await development proposals and in some cases a continuous system may never be possible. But with an overall strategy formulated at an early stage the bits and pieces of the jigsaw will eventually come together. This approach is more appropriate and in the long run will be more successful than the present hit or miss efforts where many developments are considered in isolation, and every open space is seen as an end product in itself.

SQUARES AND MARKET PLACES

As already stated the original purpose of many towns was to act as a market and service centre for the surrounding population. When such towns were first planned the squares and market places were conceived as important elements. We can compare the spaciousness, and scale of these squares with the narrowness of surrounding streets. Here major buildings are located, churches, courthouses, market houses and banks. They vary in extent and form depending on the particular town, and nature of the local topography. In the Northern towns the main square is usually called 'the Diamond'.

Today cattle and horse markets and fairs have practically disappeared and have been replaced by the ubiquitous livestock mart. Many old market places are being used as parking lots and as a dumping ground for all sorts of unwanted material. There is a need for parking, and towns that have difficulties in providing it may lose out to neighbouring towns. There must however be a

Listowel Co Kerry - The great markets and fairs are now a thing of the past, for many people just a memory. Luckily most of the squares and market places are still with us.

Above - Cobh Co Cork - This new building at a single stroke effectively destroys the scale and character of Casement Square. This Square is one of the most important spaces in Cobh, and was, up to this, largely intact.

Below - Portaferry Co Down - The fire station, public house and church, all recently built, take away from the unity of the square. This church is itself an interesting example of modern architecture but out of place in this setting. The street line, and the curved entrance to the square reflected in the other approaches should have been retained.

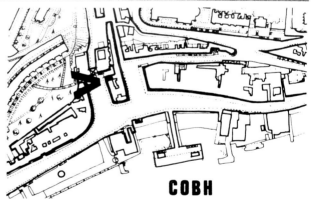

COBH

correct balance between providing for the car and retaining the architectural quality of the town. There are many ways of providing for both long and short term parking, on vacant sites awaiting redevelopment, or in back areas not so much in the public view. But a town's main square is not the most appropriate place to use as a car park.

A little imagination and care, and many squares could be improved, with additional landscaping provided, and car parking in a more orderly fashion.

There may be opportunities to carry out a comprehensive painting scheme in conjunction with a policy of removing unwanted advertisement signs, and unsightly street furniture of many kinds. Redevelopment will also provide the

Left - The Diamond Clones, Co Monaghan is a large triangular space on the top of a hill, with all the side streets leading up to it. The public toilets and information kiosk add little to its quality, and would be better located in one of the surrounding buildings.

Below - Public Toilets - The provision and siting of public toilets has for many years caused controversy in local communities, not only in Ireland but in most other countries. Often these buildings are poorly designed and badly located. The ideal public toilet should be 'accessible but not seen.'

Sixmilecross Co Tyrone may have the answer to this problem. Here a derelict house has been converted into public toilets and a bus shelter. How much better than the approach in Ballinahinch Co Down.

opportunity to insert new modern buildings which would retain the character and scale of the square. But the profile and building lines are vitally important. A single storey building in a predominantly two or three storey area could effectively ruin its character. Above all, however, squares and market places are not the areas to allow gerry building and sub-standard designs. In towns where there are a number of such spaces the relationship between them is important. One space may lead directly into another, or they may be joined together by a long street whose width and shape provides a pleasant contrast to the design and layout of the squares. This whose process of interaction between spaces is subtle and important. This will need emphasising in local townscape studies.

Right - Ballyragget Co Kilkenny - A town square is not the best place for long term parking. There are possibilities for having more attractive community uses for these spaces, and at the same time providing a certain amount of car parking.

Below - Tullow Co Carlow - The new bank building has injured the appearance of the square. The sketch shows how the use of a pitched roof would have improved matters considerably.

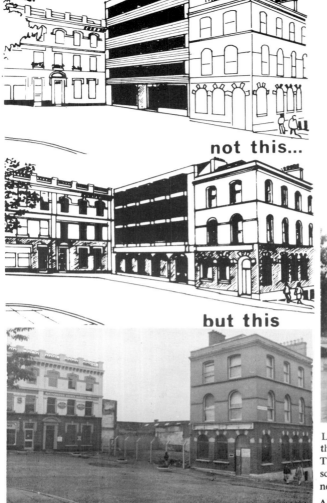

not this...

but this

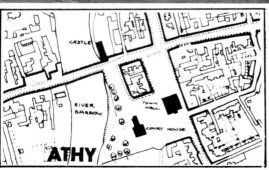

Left - - Derry City - The Diamond is the central feature of this historic city. It has suffered badly from bomb damage. There will be an opportunity for rebuilding, but the height, scale and building lines must be respected. The architecture need not necessarily be traditional.

Above - fortunately The Spinning Mill, one of the better buildings still remains.

Below - Athy Co Kildare - The town square is part of a series of spaces leading down to the River Barrow. At the moment these spaces are in danger of being taken over by motor cars and heavy trucks. It should be possible to improve the environment by reorganising the parking and planting some trees. Perhaps it would mean fewer parking spaces, but there would be a more civilised atmosphere.

Above - The Grand Canal is important to Dublin, and it is difficult to believe that only a few years ago there were serious proposals to fill in the canal and provide a 6-lane motorway in its place. This was one of Dublin's early conservation battles and it brought home to many people the need for conservation policies. It has also emphasised the importance of voluntary organisations who are prepared to assess critically, but in a positive way, major public projects. Think of what the situation would be now if this battle had been lost. The canal may have been filled in, the road would have remained unbuilt, as recent plans have considered such a road unnecessary.

Right - An example of the simple but effective detailing

CANALS AND HARBOURS

The building of canals was a great technological achievement comparable to the new techniques in present day transportation. The towns located on the canals have inherited a fine legacy of architectural and engineering works, as worthy of our concern as the better known buildings from the same period. Built in a period when design standards were quite high, these buildings have a robust quality reflected in the general use of stone and in their strong and coherent detailing. The same high design standards were also reflected in the design of the canals, locks, bridges and harbours. Transportation by canal however had a rather limited life in this country and was quickly superceded by the railways. Their use and prosperity declined and a general decay set in. Evidence of this can now be seen in nearly every canal in the country—broken locks, neglected harbours and buildings, canals choked with weeds, and in some cases filled in to provide for a road or just because it was a convenient place for

Left Top - Castletownshend Co Cork - This attractive warehouse is important visually to the harbour, and could be converted into holiday flats.

Centre - Tramore Co Waterford - The new kiosks with their clear lines, and black and white treatment have captured the atmosphere of the seaside.

Below - The same clear design expression can be found in the older cottages at Castletownshend Co Cork.

Below - The architecture of canals and harbours has a tradition for strength, beauty and functionalism. The lighthouse at Donaghadee, Co Down expresses these qualities.

dumping. But despite all these years of decay and neglect the canals, installations and buildings, still have merit and charm.

With the spectacular increase in the popularity of water based recreation, the canals, waterways, and small fishing ports generally are experiencing a renaissance. Rivers, canals and harbours now have considerable potential for development. Many older waterside buildings can be renewed to act as hostels, hotels, and so forth. Instead of being a drawback to the appearance of a town such areas now have distinct economic potential. Their rehabilitation will, however, need careful consideration. This is not the location for an over fussy or romantic style of architecture. Restoration should be done with as little change as possible to external appearances. Where there is a demand for new buildings, the architecture should be simply expressed, but sturdily and strongly detailed:

chapter 7

Living in Towns

Towns, above all else, have been places to live in. This was particularly so in Ireland, and the traditional concept of 'living over the shop' goes back a long way. Residence and work places were the same. As towns grew bigger and more complex, people not directly involved in shopping and commerce began to live in them. Areas and streets primarily residential in character developed.

Despite improvements in communications of all sorts, which makes living in the countryside more attractive, it is still highly probable that the great mass of new housing will be built in existing towns and villages. There are strong arguments in favour of this policy. Better use is made of existing capital and social investment. A wider range of services is available to the householder, such as schools, shops, community facilities. In addition there is now a common concern to conserve resources of all kinds. The energy crisis has brought this home to many people. Indiscriminate scattered developments create additional and expensive demands on land, fuel, power and public utility services.

The settlement pattern in Ireland is however so widespread and varied that restrictions on indiscriminate building in the countryside need not result in the creation of large amorphous cities as some people feel.

OLDER RESIDENTIAL AREAS

Generally, the older residential areas have considerable charm and character. There is a constraint in the use of materials and a simple dignity of approach which many new housing areas lack. The tree planting and landscaping, now mature, is attractive and adds considerably to the visual character of the town. Compare a tree lined street within the older areas with many of the new suburbs. Often the architectural details are highly original. These residential areas are also closer to shopping and community facilities and over the years have become very desirable places to live in. Strong local community cultures and identities have been established. To many people the older residential areas epitomise all that is desirable and attractive about urban living, and in this they are in marked contrast to the new housing estates. Why

Homes of charm and character are to be found in the older housing areas. They vary in scale and design, but their essential quality comes from restraint in the use of materials, varied roof lines and a general adherence to the existing street line.

this should be so is of great importance to future planning.

Why, in most instances, do the new housing estates not measure up to the quality of the older ones? Is it something to do with time and evolution; or is it that there is an obsession with rules and standards in the new housing areas and less concern with actual design and appearance. Or is it that these older residential areas are very much a part of a town which has evolved slowly over many generations, while the new housing estate may contain three to four times the population and may have developed in the space of three to four years? These are indeed fundamental questions, and to attempt to answer them would require a book in itself. The older areas are now facing problems arising out of the demands and needs of society. It is the response to these problems and the way they are tackled which contribute the main threat to their character and quality. Over the years the physical fabric has been subject to wear and tear. Changes in economic and social circumstances may have resulted in the complete decay of houses. Many are in need of renewal. The gradual developments of such areas resulted in gap sites being left over from previous developments. These now remain to be filled in.

Some of the larger houses in their own grounds are now becoming obsolete and may provide an opportunity for increased densities, but without destroying the character of the area. With the improvement in living standards there is a demand for better services and facilities, for example, bathroom and kitchen extensions. The older residential areas are therefore subject to a wide range of pressures which can and are changing their visual appearance.

Recent trends towards housing improvement and renewal is however encouraging. Many existing houses could with relatively little effort extend their life span for perhaps another forty or fifty years. This is an important fact in the context of a national housing programme and it is a trend which should get more positive encouragement and direction from local authorities and central governments. Such housing improvements will require careful visual attention. There is a tendency to increase the size of windows in an indiscriminate fashion without considering the scale of the street or the proportion of the windows in the adjoining dwellings. The need for light however is highly understandable, but with a little more thought and design this can be provided in an attractive way. The introduction of the standard casement type windows with their horizontal emphasis is rarely successful in a street where the overall design has a vertical emphasis. Better coordination between the window manufacturers and public bodies could overcome this. It should be possible for the manufacturers to produce a standard for windows more appropriate for use within older residential areas.

Building and roof lines are important and should be adhered to, within limits of course. Indeed small variations will add interest and character to the profile of the street. To provide a major break however requires careful and sensitive treatment. Generally setbacks, and flat roofs, are not happy within the context of the street scene and should be avoided.

It is important therefore that there are design standards for the rehabilitation and renewal of the older housing areas. The need for such policies is clearly evident all over the country. New buildings are erected and existing ones improved in a manner which has little in common with the overall architectural character of the town. There are many examples of what can be called 'suburban type architecture' within towns. When inserted into a street it can change its character and charm at one stroke. Unfortunately however, this type of architecture appears to be becoming more common. Perhaps we are witnessing the beginnings of a uniform and universal style of architecture, which could, in a short space of time destroy the character of our smaller towns and villages.

Planning authorities should prepare design principles to guide house-holders regarding the improvement of property. This is a sensitive task requiring care and understanding. The desire of people to improve their houses must indeed be welcome and it would be a pity if they were inhibited or prevented in any way.

Design principles however need not mean a dull uniformity for every area. With skill and imagination there will be ample opportunity for a distinctive and individual approach which will satisfy the householder but still respect the character of the area. When the opportunity for complete renewal occurs, as for example in gap sites, or where the existing property is too bad to be

Above - These houses could be restored, but if this is not possible the last thing to be considered should be a single storey suburban type bungalow. Unfortunately this is quite common in many towns.

Left - Kinsale Co Cork - The old Alms Houses before and after reconstruction.

Below - Bailieboro Co Cavan - This outbuilding has been converted into small self-contained flats, suitable for single persons and newly married couples. The architecture respects the local character.

Above - In Abbeyleix these Alms Houses form a very attractive square which unfortunately is often used for bus-parking. Some of the houses are also gone. Although the new buildings are not unpleasant they lack the character of the older ones. The remaining group should now be restored if possible, the buses removed, and the square laid out as originally conceived.

Left - New approaches to residential developments in towns.

Dalkey Co Dublin - The new houses are attractive and are a pleasant addition to the area.

Westport Co Mayo - This scheme is out of place and harms the character of this architecturally important town.

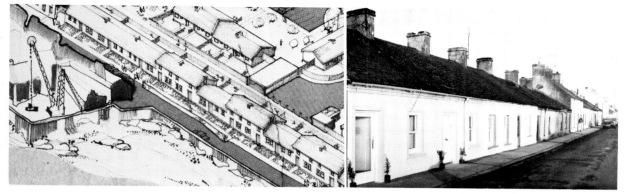

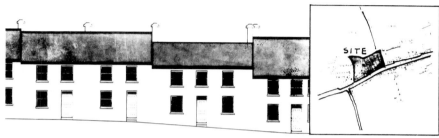

Top - Portaferry Co Down - Although it is sad that the old houses had to go, this redevelopment scheme being carried out by the Northern Ireland Housing Executive recaptures the spirit and charm of Portaferry. The street lines have been retained. The design and materials carry on the local tradition. (The old slates have been re-used).

Left - Dunmanway Co Cork - The proposals being suggested by Cork County Council for the redevelopment of this site are also in sympathy with the local character. The street line is being retained and the elevations reflect other buildings in the town.

It is pleasant to note that two public bodies at both ends of the country are now beginning to recognise that redevelopment within the existing structure of towns calls for a special approach.

Above - Cork County Council should consider the same approach in Cloyne when the rest of this street is being redeveloped. Their early essay in redevelopment is hardly in keeping with this town of strong architectural identity.

Left - Achill Island Co Mayo, old and new houses - The new house is from a standard plan produced by the Department of the Gaeltacht and it captures all the qualities of the traditional house, with its pitched roof, restrained use of material, black and white colouring. This approach, which still allows freedom for the designers, should be the norm for all new development on the Island.

renewed, the new design should relate to the street both in design and choice of material. Generally it is better if the architectural style reflects the general style in the area. In some situations there may be a case for a new architectural concept, but this will require extremely careful and sophisticated handling, and experienced architectural advice which is not always available. In the larger areas of re-development new spaces or squares can be created which will be an asset to the town.

In larger cities and towns living accommodation is being continually pushed out by the stronger economic forces of office and commercial developments. There is now a danger that the centres of the larger towns will be devoted primarily to commercial uses with little or no residential use. This has happened in American and British cities with unpleasant consequences. In the view of many people this situation has been caused by planning policies, particularly the concept of single use zoning. Therefore a policy of multi use zoning in certain parts of cities has been advocated.

Multi use zoning is a complex planning tool and indeed has in some cases resulted in less residential use rather than more. There is no doubt that a multi use area epitomised by the small town or village is more attractive both socially and visually. Here is to be found housing, shops, services, community facilities all in one unit and adjacent to each other. The older areas of the cities, 'the village within the cities' have many of the same qualities. But multi use zoning is a planning device which should be used with care. For example a zoning which would allow residential, offices and shops in a particular area might have the end result of pushing out the residential in favour of the more economically viable offices and shopping. This has been happening in parts of Dublin, particularly the Leeson Street/Ballsbridge area. It is also happening in the other large towns and cities.

Residential zoning when rigidly applied can also have bad effects. Such zoning can prohibit the development of small shops, offices, local community facilities, and give rise to the concept of the large souless housing estate, where there are no shops only large supermarkets, no small pubs but massive roadhouses surrounded by large car parks, few local facilities of any sort except at the neighbourhood centre which may be miles away.

What is really needed is zoning which takes into account the real needs of everyday life in all its facets. In certain cases it should be possible to be flexible and allow auxiliary uses such as shops and small services of a varied nature, offices and workshops, provided that they were small in scale and operation, and did not generate heavy traffic. There could be a limit to the amount of floor area occupied or the number of employees. Planners may feel that this would be difficult to operate in practice but surely one of the great problems about urban living is that the current plans, and their concern with rules and regulations, are leading to situations far removed from the social apsirations of the general public. A way must be found to rearrange administrative procedures to suit social objectives. There is as much a need if not more, for creativity in management as in other activities.

An argument often made by developers and estate agents is that a change to office use will help to prevent the physical decay of buildings. They are

Left - Dublin - Flats in the grounds of a large house - The density is increased but the scale is just right for the area.

Above - Dublin - Office Developments have taken over from living accommodation - The front gardens give way to tarmac.

Left - Cutting from a newspaper 1975 - Perhaps a portend of future policies.

Below right - The Liberties Dublin - Day long parking which destroys the amenities of the residents.

Left - Dublin - Photographed on a Sunday morning. This small residential street is very pleasant indeed, and appears quite a desirable place to live. It is close to the city centre, to community facilities, churches and schools. During working hours (centre) the street becomes a major traffic artery. Heavy trucks and vehicles of all descriptions pass through. The environment is being literally destroyed.

Lorries banned to city laneway

Mr. Justice Butler, in the High Court, Dublin, granted an injunction to John Grogan, a plumber, of 161, Richmond Road, Dublin, preventing three Dublin firms from driving heavy vehicles along a laneway at the rere of his house. The companies, James Markey Ltd., Corporation Fruit Market; Markey Prepared Food Ltd., Richmond Road, and Intertrans Ltd., Lower Gardiner Street, were also ordered to pay £300 damages and costs.

Mr. Grogan had complained that the companies had used the laneway since June, 1972, driving large lorries, trailers and articulated trucks by his house, resulting in damage to it because of their size and weight.

The court ordered that the companies must not use the laneway for vehicles exceeding 10 tons in weight and 24 feet in length.

usually referring to areas where houses are quite large, and related to a past life style when servants were common. Their argument is, that office and commercial users generally have more money available for maintenance and the houses are looked after properly. But is this generally the case? The first signs of a change in an area from residential to office use is usually the removal of railings, the uprooting of the front garden, changing it into a car park. The houses are much more intensively used, there is additional weight on the floors and there are many more occupants per square foot.

In recent years the problem of traffic has created many difficulties for people living in the older residential districts. Because of proximity to the major commercial and industrial areas these streets have had to bear the brunt of traffic congestion of many sorts. They have become parking lots for nearby shopping streets, and have been turned into one-way speedways to facilitate traffic management schemes, the major objective of which is to speed up traffic flow, irrespective of environmental or other consequences. This is one of the main reasons for people leaving such areas, and emphasises a major flash point in urban conservation. Are towns to be planned for the motor car or for people? Residents of such streets may accept their own or their neighbour's car parked outside the door, but when their street is turned into a mass car park all day long this constitutes a real loss of environmental standards. It does of course represent an easy way out for the local authority who should be providing more adequate parking facilities. However even when facilities are provided, motorists are reluctant to use them, and often resort to the nearest street irrespective of the inconvenience caused to the residents.

The problems are even greater when such streets become traffic highways because of a traffic management scheme. Not only motor vehicles but 'juggernaut' lorries now rumble through residential streets. The very size and weight of these huge lorries will cause structural problems which are a financial burden on the occupants of these houses. They also cause pollution from fumes, noise and vibrations.

In theory the only traffic which should be allowed into a residential street is that which may have some business there. All other traffic should be barred. This is difficult to work in practice. It will require much wider and tougher enforcement, as well as the provision of adequate parking facilities elsewhere in the town.

There is a very strong case to be made for preventing heavy lorries from using a residential street. Perhaps they should even be fined for doing so. Devices such as 'rumble strips'* can act as a deterrent, and would at least cut down on excessive speeds. In the absence of policies of this sort the environmental qualities of the older residential areas will be continuously eroded.

NEW HOUSING AREAS

The physical expansion of towns has up to now taken the form of new housing estates. Such estates invariably have the same appearance whether they are in a small village or a large city. Located mainly on the outskirts, they form amorphous sprawls eating into the countryside, at the same time they add little to the quality and character of the town. The design of new housing is however

These are humps in the street designed to slow down traffic.

86

Top - Tallaght Co Dublin and Trim Co Meath - Obviously something has gone serious wrong when such notices have to be erected in a new housing estate. The reason of course is that far too many housing estates have been built with the needs of the motor car in mind and the pedestrian is completely ignored.

This alone is a strong reason for reconsidering the present approach to housing design and layout.

Above - Typical view of a new housing estate - It is hard for residents to identify with an environment like this.

Left - pleasant new housing at Donaghadee Co Down. The importance of retaining existing trees in new housing estates is often overlooked elsewhere. It would take many generations for new trees to reach this size.

87

a very complex problem and is outside the scope of this particular book. The present scale of expansion is enormous. In Dublin alone the population is forecast to increase by over half a million people over the next twenty years. This will be in the form of new housing areas, of generally low density, on what is now agricultural land. All the present indications are that the dread hand of uniformity is spreading over the country. The same monotonous layout of detached and semi-detached houses are being used indiscriminately in town and village. The layouts appear to reflect engineering principles, regarding road widths, sight lines, turning space for refuse vehicles, rather than architectural requirements.

There are unfortunately few examples of really good quality private housing estates. Standards of design and layout are generally much better for public housing. There is less concern with pure economic returns, certainly more use is made of professional advisors. It should be possible to create new housing areas which would contribute to the architectural character of the town and its general environmental quality. In achieving this the quality and layout is more important than the detailed design of individual houses. New housing areas should be closely integrated with the town centre by the use of open spaces, footpaths and pedestrian ways. This can be achieved by selecting the most appropriate sites to build on, rather than developing areas where acquisition is easy. It is quite common to see housing estates built at some distance from the centre of the town while the intervening areas remain undeveloped, increasing its value for the private individual at the expense of the community.

Limavady Co Derry - This new housing scheme is quite successful in many ways. The old railway line has been converted into an open space, A pleasant atmosphere has been created by the careful use of materials on a domestic scale.

There is a pleasant contrast between the paved inner courts and the open atmosphere of the park.

There are a number of planning principles which if followed could improve the environmental quality within the new areas.

1.   There should be a pleasant and safe environment. This will mean that the needs of the residents are given priority over traffic. Busy traffic routes should be separated from access roads to housing, and from the major pedestrian ways. The housing area should be conceived as a totally integrated community where traffic, landscaping, land use, are part of an overall conception, and not planned in a piecemeal manner.

2.   All existing items of interest in an area; the planting, views, existing settlement pattern; areas of historical, architectural, archaeological and landscape importance should not only be preserved but, more importantly, incorporated in a positive and imaginative way into the scheme. There is not much point in preserving an old church, or group of trees if for example they are located in the middle of a traffic roundabout and bear little relationship to the development adjacent to them. A feeling of continuity, respect for traditions, can therefore be in-built into a new community, the new residents may then more easily feel a sense of belonging, and this will help them to quickly establish their own roots.

3.   The provision of community and social facilities must keep pace with population growth. It may even be necessary to reduce the population growth to some extent in order to provide a balance between growth and the provision of social and community facilities. There are too many examples in the past of major housing developments which for a generation or so had only the minimum of facilities, and in some cases none at all.

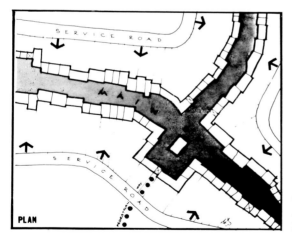

PLAN

Squares and Streets are basic design forms which have given pleasure to generations of town dwellers. Let us not be afraid of creating these spaces in new development areas. Instead of building sterile shopping centres why not attempt to recreate the old streets with a mixture of shops, offices and housing, with servicing and access at the back. They could be built in individual units or in small groups. The Local Authority could have an overall design concept covering materials, building lines, heights, land use, traffic and services.

ELEVATION OF MAIN STREET

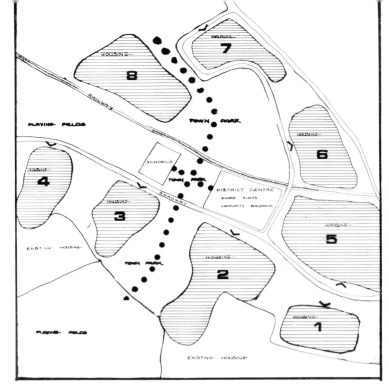

New housing development Limerick City - In this scheme there are a number of clearly defined and distinct housing areas. These areas will not be affected by through traffic, and each can have a different design expression. They could evolve into small village type communities with their own individual atmosphere. Open spaces and recreational areas serve as a link joining the housing areas together.

4.   In design terms, a human scale is absolutely vital. Social research has established that within large cities the older and closely-knit communities are in fact villages within the city. In such situations social attitudes are healthier, and there is less vandalism than in the new sprawling estates. Planners and architects should therefore create a climate whereby similar type communities can evolve and develop in new housing areas. Each housing group should have a clearly expressed physical identity. There should be no through traffic. It should have a central focal point: a small green or open space, with social facilities such as shops, school, nursery school and community centre. The different housing groups should be linked together physically by open spaces, and each should have good access to the town centre and to employment, recreation and amenity areas. In the larger developments, housing groups should, as a general rule, contain no more than 100–150 houses and a population of 400/600 persons, –the size of a village. A series of groups could provide a neighbourhood.

5.   The focal point of the neighbourhoods should be the centre, incorporating primary school, town park, shops, churches and community facilities. There should also be land preserved for ancillary uses, the demand for which may not be apparent until the houses are occupied and the community begins to develop. These centres should be allowed to evolve in an organic way with smaller type shops and public houses with residential accommodation overhead, thereby creating the atmosphere of a small town. They should not be subject to rigid zoning regulations. The reserve sites could be used for service functions, for example, offices, light industry, provided they did not generate too much traffic. Each centre should have its own distinctive character and appearance.

chapter 8

Traffic in Towns

Towns by their very nature generate traffic of all sorts. They are centres of commerce, employment, and contain social and community facilities. This has always been the case, and in the past, also, there have been traffic problems. However, these have been of a relatively local nature, occurring mainly on market and fair days. Commerce was locally orientated, commercial goods were carried over longer distances by the railways.

Towns have now to accommodate very different activities than in the last century, or for that matter a few decades ago. The increase of white collar and service employment, the centralization of more and more power into fewer and fewer centres, has resulted in the growth of the large cities and towns, with their tremendous traffic problems.

In recent years, therefore, the growth of traffic in towns and the problems caused by it have become one of the great issues in urban conservation all over the world. There is a direct contradiction between an uninhibited and unlimited use of the motor car and the environmental quality of the towns, particularly the older parts. These areas were designed and built before the motor car was even dreamt of. Since then there have been vast social and economic changes. The motor car has now become a dominant feature of our modern life. The physical fabric of towns has, however, remained essentially the same. There are narrow shopping streets, a variety of land uses, areas of architecural character, and historic importance. These have now to accommodate motor traffic of all sorts.

It is obviously not possible to meet such demands and retain any semblance of character and quality in our towns. The motor car is one of the great social paradoxes of our times. On the one hand it offers great mobility previously undreamt of. Remote areas are within an hour's drive from major downs and cities. The country dweller has now a wider range of facilities available to him. However traffic can by its danger, noise, fumes, vibration and visual intrusion literally destroy the physical character of towns, and the quality of life within them.

A feature of planning over the last decade has been an over emphasis on traffic matters. Traffic planning was considered as an end in itself. This is of

Above left - Drogheda - one of the most congested towns in the country. It can sometimes take up to an hour to pass through the town.

Some years ago when a by-pass was first muted there was vigorous opposition on the grounds that the town would lose out financially. In recent years there has been pressure to provide another bridge over the River Boyne and by-pass the centre. This proposal is now being implemented.

Right - Hillsborough Co Down - Another town on the same road which had been badly affected by traffic. The by-pass is now in operation, and heavy traffic no longer goes through the town centre.

Left - Sneem Co Kerry - It has been suggested that this attractive bridge be widened or replaced because of traffic requirements.

Surely in this pleasant village this is the last thing that should happen. The bridge is a vital part of Sneem's architectural character, and links the two squares together. It also regulates, and slows down, the traffic in the village.

Below - Cavan Town - What was previously a pleasant open space in the centre has been developed as a used car lot. This happened some time ago. One hopes it would not be allowed under the present planning laws.

93

course contrary to the real life situation. Traffic is but one aspect of a town's planning problem, and it cannot be tackled in isolation. Traffic studies for many of the larger towns have been prepared. Many grandiose recommendations have been made, but to date very little has been achieved. With the increasing cost of motor transport it appears as if the age of the 'big traffic scheme', particularly in towns, is at an end.

By contrast, very few detailed studies of the architectural qualities of towns have been undertaken. For example, there have been traffic plans prepared for towns of major architectural importance such as Wexford and Kilkenny, but to date no official study of the rich and varied architectural heritage of these towns has been carried out.

The Architectural School from the College of Technology in Bolton Street, Dublin, has prepared extremely interesting and comprehensive townscape studies of both Wexford and Kilkenny. These could form the basis for an official policy.

Up to quite recently, the general approach was to plan for, and to accommodate, the motor car. This was expressed by the philosophy — 'the car is here to stay, there is nothing we can do about it. People having acquired cars must be allowed to use them irrespective of what congestion and danger they might cause to others.' Such an approach produced the major traffic schemes for cities and towns. In the cities new motor ways were planned, and some built, causing vast disruption to homes and property, and requiring an enormous amount of expenditure to implement. And in the end, if we can judge from the experience in other countries, such policies have not really solved the traffic problems. They did, however, give rise to major social problems. Older communities in the inner areas of the cities were literally destroyed to allow for the motor car.

The same situations are beginning to arise in Ireland. Both the Dublin and Belfast traffic plans, if implemented in full, would have disrupted a number of long established and closely knit communities. In the case of Belfast, the Sandy Row area and in the case of Dublin, the Liberties and a number of dock side communities. These proposals are meeting with great opposition because the general public have now reached the conclusion that the philosophy of planning for the unlimited use of the motor car in the cities has not been successful.

At the other end of the scale similar techniques have been adopted. In the smaller towns there are policies to provide for the widening of existing streets. New buildings when being erected are set back from the existing building line, to provide for road widening at some point in the distant future. Streets are thus often widened in a piecemeal manner, irrespective of any visual considerations or traffic dangers they might cause in other parts of the town.

The policy of widening streets in an ad hoc manner appears to be in the final analysis illogical. It contributes very little to easing the traffic situation as a whole. This policy can destroy the character of towns for the needs of the traffic. Fortunately this approach to the traffic problems is becoming more unacceptable to local communities, who now realise that often the 'cure is much worse than the disease'.

In the larger towns traffic management schemes have been adopted to

Below - Jamestown Co Leitrim - The arch was important historically and environmentally to the village. Jamestown lost an important part of its history when the arch was demolished. What was Jamestown's gain? Nothing, except a faster flow of heavy traffic through the village. It deserves better than this.

ove - Kilmallock Co Limerick - The gates at mallock provide an exciting entrance into town. They also help to slow traffic down perhaps more importantly, are a physical ninder of the town's varied and exciting ory.

There has been talk in recent years of molishing the gates, again in order to wide for heavy through traffic.

It is hoped that the mistake in Jamestown not be repeated in Kilmallock.

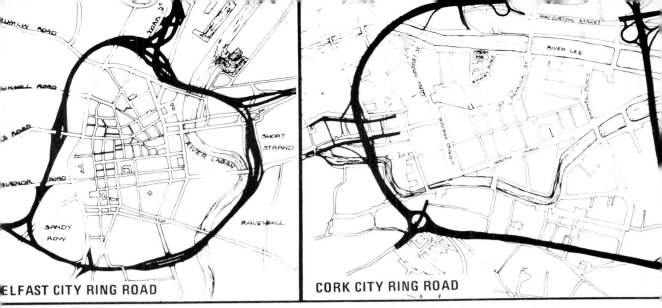

ELFAST CITY RING ROAD

CORK CITY RING ROAD

The Belfast Traffic study caused much controversy because of its effects on closely knit, and long standing, communities.

This type of scheme can cause considerable planning blight, as invariably new development adjacent to the proposed routes is restricted until the facilities have been designed in detail. Usually little attention is paid to pedestrian movement, land use requirements, public transport or civic design matters.

The 1968 Cork Traffic Study proposed an inner distributor road. This was to be a six-lane motorway, elevated in parts, and encircling the city centre. Within this area many existing streets were to be widened. It was originally intended that the entire scheme be completed by 1986. The scheme involved extensive acquisition and demolition of property, and much disruption of housing.

facilitate the movement of traffic. This may have required a restriction on turning in certain directions, or one-way streets diverting more traffic on to adjacent roads. Initially, this sort of approach does increase traffic flow, but almost invariably it is at the expense of the environmental quality in other parts of the town and in particular the residential areas. Streets and squares, many of them of a pleasant and attractive character, have been literally taken over by parked vehicles.

However motor traffic is a fact of modern life and cannot be wished away. The plans being proposed for cities and towns have to recognise, and come to terms with this situation. On the other hand the architectural quality of our towns, and in addition the quality of life within them, should not be destroyed by a blind submission to the needs of the motor car. There is a real conflict here which planning authorities working in co-operation with the local community must resolve. In the cities a whole new philosophy is needed. More stringent restrictions on the use of the motor car will be necessary. Increased investment in public transport systems of many kinds will be required as opposed to more investments in roads. A new approach to movements within the city centre, perhaps using such items as mini-buses, improved taxi services, and even free transport will be required in some situations.

The Dublin bus strike in 1974 must surely have emphasised beyond all doubt that in the larger cities an adequate public transport system is an indispensable part of the financial structure of city centres. City centres will not die without an investment in new roads, but the Dublin strike proved that they could die without a public transport system. From all accounts during this

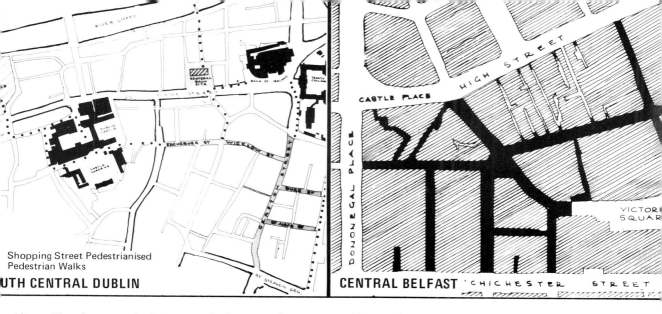

Shopping Street Pedestrianised
Pedestrian Walks

UTH CENTRAL DUBLIN

CENTRAL BELFAST

Above - There is an opportunity to create in the centre of
Dublin an area where the pedestrian would have precedence
over traffic. The more important shopping streets and major
public buildings on both sides of the river could be linked.
It would not necessarily be a traffic free area. There would
be a need to provide for servicing of premises, and for public
transport. The pavements could be widened, and major
pedestrian crossings formed, to link in other public buildings
on the periphery of the area, for example Trinity College.

Above - A large part of the centre of Belfast is now traffic
free for security reasons.

The Royal Society of Ulster Architects has sponsored
a study, arguing the case that the traffic free area should
be continued on a permanent basis. It is now probable
that their proposals will be implemented in some form or
another.

Left - Henry Street Dublin before the traffic was removed
- Compare the situation to-day.

Below Left - Grafton Street Dublin during the short time
when it was traffic free - Compare also the situation
to-day.

Below - The central square in Athlone has the potential
of becoming an attractive area with the church and
grounds as its dominant feature. Unfortunately it is now
ruined by through traffic.

There is the possibility of a relief road. What a
difference this would make!

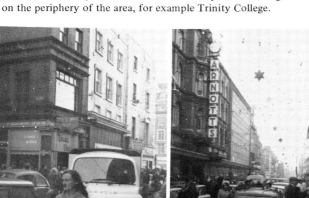

97

ARECASTLE CO. CLARE

Above - Clarecastle Co Clare - The buildings which help to define the corner are now gone. The character of the town has been changed. There are now a number of possibilities.
A. Convert the area into a car park and leave the gap as it is now or:-
B. Develop the site providing housing and shops with a car park behind.
    With a sensitive building the character and qualify of the village will be improved, and community facilities provided at the same time.

Left - Newtownards Co Down - Public parking in the best location, behind the main streets - not in view but accessible to all the main activities.

Below - Newtownards Co Down - The central square which is the main feature of the town has been closed to traffic for security reasons. It is now the intention of the local council to make this a permanent feature.

strike, trade and social life in the city centre declined disastrously. This decline began to affect employment, not only in the city centre shops but throughout the country in the factories and workshops.

In most Irish towns, however, sophisticated traffic management schemes, or extensive public transport facilities will not be feasible or economical. The larger concentrations of populations in Ireland are generally located on the coastline, and major roads radiate out from these centres. Many towns and villages are located on busy roads connecting the major cities and towns. Commercial goods are generally carried by road and more and more by the larger transport vehicles — 'the juggernaut lorries'. Indeed pressures are building up from the Continent to allow even larger vehicles on our roads. Over the years it may be difficult to resist these pressures. It has been estimated that an investment of up to 500 million pounds will be required to make the roads in the Republic suitable for the big continental transport vehicles. The very existence of these vehicles constitutes a real threat to the quality of life in towns. They can be seen rumbling through the shopping streets of towns causing disruption and chaos with their noise and fumes. Some towns are being destroyed by commercial traffic, the greater percentage of which has no business in the town except that it is travelling from one destination to another and must travel through certain towns on the way.

The increase in the size of road transport vehicles and the tremendous problems caused by them may now be a blessing in disguise. It should force local authorities to tackle the traffic problems in a more comprehensive manner. By far the most satisfactory way to resolve this problem is to provide a by-pass. In the past however, the mere mention of a by-pass was enough to spark off controversy and arouse emotional issues of all sorts. Commercial interests often considered that a by-pass would mean economic ruin and disaster. Many sound and necessary schemes have been postponed because of this fear. Indeed when being discussed they were called circular routes, ring roads, tangential roads, but never a by-pass. The business people considered a town primarily as a commercial unit and secondly a place for living in. In fact it is both.

However, the tremendous increase in traffic with its obvious problems and dangers has brought home to many people the need for by-passes. Even the traders are now aware that the amount of business to be gained from through traffic is quite small in comparison to their overall turnover. Traffic congestion is in fact making it more difficult for the local residents to shop and go about their business. As a result trade is now being lost. The traffic and congestion problems in some of the larger towns, give rise to pressures for out of town shopping areas. Such centres can disrupt the whole economic balance of the town, and quickly lead to the decline of the traditional town centre.

In the smaller towns and villages the need for a by-pass is equally pressing, not so much from an economic, but from an environmental point of view. Heavy trucks and fast cars speeding through a village can make living intolerable. The few towns that have been by-passed demonstrate the rise in environmental qualities achieved by this device.

Where by-passes are being provided, a land use policy is also important. The by-pass road should be kept free from all development. There is no point in the world in providing a by-pass for a town and then allowing major commercial activities to locate beside it. This will defeat the whole purpose of the by-pass, cause even additional traffic hazards, and also disrupt the economic life of the town. In market towns when the through traffic is taken away it should be easier to deal with local traffic and plan for this without destroying the character of the town.

In larger cities the problem is more complex. In addition to a by-pass the sheer volume of traffic may also necessitate a relief road to the main shopping streets and central areas. The problems caused by purely local traffic can also make conditions difficult and dangerous, this has led to the pedestrianisation of shopping streets.

Where this has been carried out it has improved conditions generally. Initially such suggestions aroused misgivings and doubts, particularly on the part of the traders. However experience to date has shown that trade does not suffer and may even improve. Henry Street in Dublin is a more pleasant street

Kill Co Kildare - The by-pass road has effectively raised the environmental quality of the village. Many towns and villages could be by-passed, and evidence to date has shown that there is little economic loss.

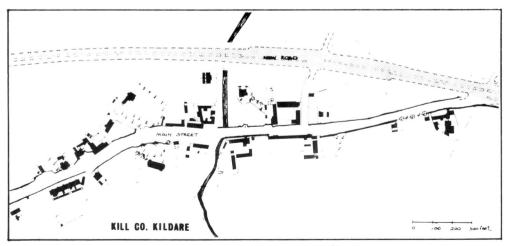

KILL CO. KILDARE

since the traffic was removed and is as busy as ever. Grafton Street, Dublin, when the traffic was removed was a pleasant contrast to the fume ridden street it is now. Surely it makes common sense to pedestrianise this street on a permanent basis.

Many cities and towns in Europe have pedestrian-only streets, and the trend is increasing. The supreme example is, of course, Venice whose traffic free streets help to make it one of the most memorable and exciting of cities. In Ireland there are fewer examples yet, but there are many streets where conditions would be considerably improved by pedestrianisation, even if it were only for a few hours during the busy shopping days.

Pedestrianisation, however, to be highly successful should be conceived as part of an overall plan where a large area may be gradually pedestrianised. Such areas would include not only one shopping street but a number of streets, squares, parks, residential streets, all building up into a comprehensive and integrated unit.

1961

Fears Of Naas By-Pass Allayed

THERE is no present intention of by-passing Naas. An assurance to this effect was given by the Kildare County Manager, Mr. M. Macken, on Friday. He was replying to a deputation from Naas Chamber of Commerce. This body had viewed with apprehension a report that the town would be by-passed, and the question has been of particular concern to the members since the Chamber was formed.

The deputation was appointed at the Chamber's last meeting and was instructed to ask the County Manager to use all his influence to ensure that by-passing would not materialise. Mr. Macken's assurance was received with great relief, a sentiment echoed throughout the town.

Mr. Macken said that while the design of the dual carriageway was such as to make it possible to construct a by-pass in the future should traffic congestion in the town make it absolutely necessary, there was at present no intention of constructing a by-pass.

It was the policy of the County Council to improve the road system and parking within the town so that the necessity for a by-pass would be avoided as long as possible. This policy was also being pursued in relation to other towns such as Athy and Kildare.

The question the deputation asked him was this—was it the intention of the authorities, in his opinion, to by-pass the town of Naas?

He was further queried on what was the exact authority which would order the by-pass to be carried out—was it the County Council, or was it the Department of Local Government on the recommendation of the County Council, or did the Government have the complete authority?

To this Mr. Macken replied that while the County Council was the road authority for the county, it might well be that eventually a national road authority might have to be formed should opposition to this type of road development grow to great proportions.

The deputation was: Messrs. Ger. Grehan, Eddie Marum, Tom Dowling,

J. Carina, Michael Keenan (President), Harry Hillock (Secretary), and Patrick Fitzsimons.

They pointed out that every step should be taken to improve the flow of traffic through the town by modifying the approaches and doing any other necessary works to control traffic.

Mr. Macken, having emphasised the point that the County Council was doing all it could towards this end, said that for his own part he had never experienced any difficulty in getting through the town or finding parking space for his car.

Mr. Hillock said that more than twenty-five per cent of the town's trade was from passing traffic. Naas, to a great extent, he added, had been built up on this trade and was more dependant on it than any other provincial town of which he was aware.

Other points made by the deputation were that the loss of this trade would be felt particularly by caterers, owners of licensed premises and garages. Unemployment would certainly ensue, it was claimed, and the valuation of property drop.

The policy of every political party and national voluntary organisation was to prevent emigration by preserving rural amenities, said the delegation, and the by-passing of county towns like Naas was the very negation of this policy.

ABOUT £2 MILLION

Work on the scheme to link Naas and Dublin by dual carriageway—the whole foundation for fears of a by-pass of Naas —began about twelve months ago and several long stretches appear near completion. The cost is expected to be about £2 million which is wholly a national charge.

At the time constructional work started it was estimated that, allowing for funds continuing to be available, three or four years should see it through.

The cost to be borne by County Kildare ratepayers directly will be almost negligible. They will have to pay

Youthful Knocknadruce Winner

Evidence of the changing public attitudes towards the question of traffic in towns.

In the 1960's this attitude was understandable, because the dangers both economically and physically were not fully appreciated.

1973

29/9/73 Leinster Leader

NAAS BY-PASS PLANS UP FOR APPROVAL

PLANS FOR THE proposed by-pass of Naas have been sent to the Department of Local Government for approval, the Town Clerk, Mr. P. J. Gavin, told Naas U.D.C. meeting.

During a discussion on traffic problems in the town, Clr. T. G. Dowling said big lorries were going through the town with loads not properly tied down. The noise was dreadful and the smell of some of them was foul. People were getting sick on the streets from the smells.

Clr. Mrs. Healy proposed that the Minister be asked to do something about the problem.

Clr. Dowling said the lorries should not be allowed through the Main Street.

Clr. G. Grehan, Chairman, referred to lorries emitting black smoke. The drivers were seldom prosecuted for this offence, he claimed.

The Town Clerk said that the Gardai had informed the Council that they could prosecute and were paying special attention to the problem.

Clr. Dowling said Basin Street should be made one-way.

The Town Clerk said a by-pass was the only answer and plans had been sent to the Department for approval.

Chairman: I think money is the trouble there.

Mr. J. J. Mullaney, Acting County Manager: I agree.

Continuing, the Chairman said by-pass was the only long-term solution. They could adopt some interim measures such as asking the Gardai to make Basin Street and Michael's Terrace one-way streets.

Clr. Mrs. Healy suggested a footbridge be erected, and the Chairman said the Council's policy was to erect lights.

Farmers and income tax

County Kildare I.F.A. Executive resolution on income tax adopted last week does not rule out payment of rates entirely. A spokesman said this week, on a point of clarification that the agreeableness of Kildare farmers to pay income tax if relieved of rates applied merely their means of livelihood, the land.

They were quite prepared to continue paying rates on residences and on buildings on the land, it was emphasised, but felt the land should be exempted from rates if they were to pay income tax. A readiness by farmers to contribute their share like the rest of the community, the Exchequer is embodied in the thinking behind the resolution, the spokesman stressed.

Plans for all major towns and cities should include for such an eventuality. Therefore when the redevelopment of certain buildings and areas occurs it will be possible to improve the means of vehicle access and allow at the same time a further stage of the pedestrian process to be implemented. Even without waiting for some far distant date when such policies can be completed, there are other approaches which can now be adopted which will improve the situation. Shopping streets can be closed to traffic for a few hours per day. Squares and open spaces could perhaps be closed to traffic at weekends and at holidays and festival times. Indeed there are many opportunities for imaginative and creative management.

At the present time, for security reasons, the central areas of most Northern towns have been closed to all but essential traffic. While this is not an ideal situation to measure the impact on trade and commerce, there is a general feeling that when the security situation returns to normal some restrictions on traffic should remain.

Dromore Co Down (population 3,500 approx) - An Historic town with narrow streets. For years its environment was spoiled by heavy traffic on the Dublin/Belfast road. To-day it is by-passed. The central area is a much more pleasant place.

The residents, and people from the adjacent countryside can now carry out their business in comfort and safety. Trade has not declined.

This should be a lesson for other similar sized towns in the country.

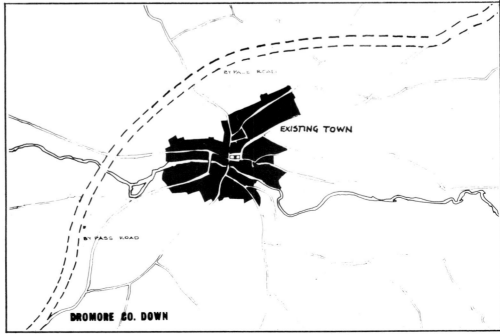

DROMORE CO. DOWN

chapter9

Buildings of Interest

South Abby

Practically every town will have some particular buildings of importance to its physical character. They may be important because of use, function, historical association, or the intrinsic quality of their architecture. Other buildings although not particularly important in themselves are by their position in the town of townscape importance. These may be situated at corners or located at other focal points in the town. Ill conceived changes to the appearance of this type of building can do lasting damage to the quality of a town.

The first category , churches, market houses, court houses, schools and public buildings of various types because of their function are often located in strategic positions in the town. They are generally part of the original fabric of the town, and so are specially important. In the 18th century the siting and design of public buildings was considered to be of great importance. As a general rule their architectural quality is high. In some instances it can be measured in national or even international terms. More usually however it is important in relation to the local scene.

CHURCHES

Churches are most common among public buildings. In nearly every town of any size there will be a Catholic, Church of Ireland, and Presbyterian Church, and indeed quite often churches belonging to other denominations. Their spires are important visually to the town, and can also be seen from some distance out in the countryside.

The actual relationship of church to the surrounding area can vary. Usually they are situated apart from other buildings in densely planted grounds. The buildings create a focal point for the town, and the spacious grounds add a softening effect to the street. In many of the smaller villages they are the most important visual element. In other instances, particularly in the larger towns, churches are more closely integrated into the street scene, and here their elevational treatment makes an interesting contrast to the surrounding buildings. However, churches too are affected by modern developments. Congregations are diminishing or amalgamating with other churches. As a result many churches are now obsolete. They present a sorry

Page 103 - Top Kiltegan Co Wicklow, Centre - John's Square Limerick, Bottom - Courthouse Carlow

Churches - The relationship of a church to a town may vary from place to place. Invariably, however, the spire or tower is visually important.

Top - Sometimes the importance of the churches are emphasised in the plan form as in Enniskillen Co Fermanagh and Tyrellspass Co Westmeath.

Bottom left - A church by its very position and scale can dominate a town, as in Cobh Co Cork.

Bottom right - In other instance the effect will be more subtle, but just as effective. The church may form part of the street elevation, and its facade will usually make a pleasant contrast to the surrounding buildings, as in St. Catherine's Church Dublin.

sight — doors closed, paintwork peeling, gutters broken — prime examples of urban decay and change. The buildings however are often structurally sound. These churches are important visually and historically. It is important therefore that a use should be found for these churches which would enhance their appearance and be consistent with their original function. With comparatively little effort they can make admirable exhibition halls and community centres.

Ennis Co Clare - The former Presbyterian Church and Manse have been successfully incorporated into a new complex, providing a library, museum and art gallery.

There are many other examples throughout the country where disused churches have been successfully converted. There are many more, however, awaiting a new use.

MARKET HOUSES AND COURTHOUSES

Nearly every town in the country would have had a market house. They were important to the economic life of the town, and were usually sited in a significant position. Very few are now being used for their original purpose. Some are being allowed to decay, while many have been needlessly destroyed. Others have been disfigured to serve a modern function and are beyond restoration. Examine the older ordnance survey maps and compare them with the situation now. Mountrath Co Laois ,Dunmanway Co Cork,Ballinasloe Co Galway have lost their market houses. This has happened during a period when there was little understanding or appreciation of their significance. During this time a number came into private ownership, but these have suffered visually.

A few market houses, such as in Kildare Town and Portaferry Co Down, have been successfully restored and given an appropriate modern use. Many however still remain more or less in their original state. With a little effort and imagination they could be re-adapted and used as a museum, exhibition hall or information centre. Indeed many towns lack these facilities, and would benefit from such a conversion.

Courthouses vary considerably in design depending on their size and particular function. In the smaller towns and villages they are of course small and reflect the general character of the town. In the larger towns, where the most important cases are decided, the courthouses are generally imposing

The Market House in Kildare Town which has been successfully restored.

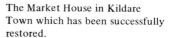

Market House at Gort Co Galway - An extremely attractive building which merges successfully into the street elevation.

Below - The Market House at Portaferry Co Down has been successfully restored and is now used for community purposes.

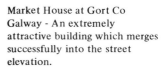

107

buildings, sited with care, and designed to grand classical proportions. A number are of national architectural importance. In most towns they are still used for their original purpose and indeed recently have combined the function of both courthouse and local authority office. In these cases they are maintained in a reasonable condition, but there are instances from time to time of Judges refusing to sit in courthouses because of their poor condition. Although the buildings themselves may be well maintained, too often the surroundings and grounds do not reflect their quality. There are many opportunities for town improvement lost here.

With the trend of local authorities to move into more suitable purpose built offices and with the courts becoming influenced by the centralisation process which is such a feature of modern life, it would appear that many courthouses may soon be obsolete, and looking for a new role.

Both market houses and courthouses have been important in the life of Irish towns. They are so numerous, so varied in their architecture, and have such obvious historical links with local life and culture, that they would justify more intensive research. To date little has been done apart from C.E. Brett's interesting book on *The Courthouses and Market Houses of Ulster*. The other Provinces await a similar study. If such buildings are restored and improved, it will help the visual character of the town and also give it a sense of history and continuity so important in this age of rapid change.

In considering new uses for such buildings two important points should be remembered. Firstly the buildings cannot be separated from the spaces around them. They are part of the same design conception. An important public building loses some of its dignity when surrounded by a sea of tarmac. There must be a balance between the character and dignity of a building and the need to provide facilities, for example car parking. Secondly, the interior design and treatment should if possible reflect the atmosphere of the building. It is always a sad sight to find a public building with the exterior intact, but with the interior mutilated beyond recognition.

CASTLES AND ESTATE HOUSES

In earlier times the importance of the local chief was identified by the castle, which was located in the town itself if it was of military or economic significance. Many castles still remain and are important both architecturally and historically. They also have potential from a tourist, and therefore economic, point of view. In some instances they are now in ruins and cannot easily be adapted to new uses. But their ruinous state is a valid expression of their history, and more relevant because of this. In other places the castles have been restored and are now a feature of the town as for example Kilkenny, Cahir Co Tipperary, and Carrickfergus Co Antrim.

Traditionally towns have been associated with a local landlord who lived in the 'big house'. But even if the house itself is not an important element in the physical structure of the town, the grounds, which are invariably of high-landscape quality, can be a vital part of its natural setting.

Here again there is functional change. Large houses are expensive to run and maintain, and many have been converted, some successfully, into hotels or

1

3

3

2

4

1. Frenchpark Co Roscommon - market house worthy of conservation.
2. The Market House of Portarlington Co Laois - before being disfigured by advertisements.

3. The Market House at Monaghan is being used as a store and is usually surrounded by parked cars; it deserves better.
4. Mountrath Co Laois - The market house was demolished to make way for a traffic roundabout.

Left - Courthouse Birr Co Offaly - Buildings like this cannot be separated from their surroundings, boundary walls and railings are an essential part of the design.

These remarks are equally relevant to many other Courthouses, but particularly Carlow (See page 103)

Below Left - Portarlington Co Laois - These new public buildings totally ignore a long standing tradition of good civic architecture in Irish towns.

schools without any great loss of quality. Others however have suffered drastically in the process mainly due to a lack of understanding or appreciation of the problems involved. In any future developments it is important therefore that the architectural quality of the houses and the visual quality of the landscape are not sacrificed for short term gains.

'Town houses' formerly belonging to the more prosperous merchants and professional classes are to be found in the larger towns. Again there are problems of structural decline and functional obsolescence and it is necessary to find new uses which do not destroy their character. They are generally built in terraces, and conceived as a unit. A change of use or any structural improvements must recognise the overall unit of the group. A policy of preservation with regard to the facades will generally be the most acceptable approach. Only if an entire block was being replaced might a new design conception be successful. The individual buildings in these terraces are in reality only an element of the overall unit, comparable to say the doors or windows of a detached building. Make an insensitive change and you destroy the entire character.

All the buildings in this first category have one thing in common. They are generally recognised as being of importance either to the architectural character of the town or its history. Therefore they should be listed as being worthy of preservation in the local development plan. But listing a building for preservation and ensuring that it is going to be restored and properly used are two quite different and distinct things.

Here is a problem fundamental to the whole question of urban conservation. There is little point in listing areas, or buildings as being worthy of perservation, if no positive attempts are made to ensure that the buildings are made structurally sound, and also acquire new uses. Experience from many countries has established that the mere listing of a building is at best only a help towards its preservation. There are examples of listed buildings being demolished, allowed to fall into such decay that restoration is well nigh impossible.

The ideal approach of course is that buildings worthy of preservation should be integrated in a positive and meaningful way into the life and activity of the town. It makes little sense to make a preservation order for a group of town houses if at the same time they are allowed to wither and decay, or indeed on the other hand in restoring an important building such as a church if it is then situated in the middle of a traffic roundabout, or completely unrelated to its surroundings. This problem is however common all over Europe, and one of the principal objectives of European Architectural Heritage Year has been not only to prevent buildings being demolished or needlessly disfigured, but to find 'new uses for old buildings'. Uses which can reflect social needs and requirements and also respect their architectural character. What is urgently needed is a fresh approach by governments and local authorities to urban conservation. A system of improved financial grants for listed buildings, for example a rates subsidy, or in certain cases a direct grant to help towards maintenance. Where extensive restoration is being carried out, which might also have social and community benefits, for example the provision of housing, or a community centre, an extra grant over and above the

Top - King John's Castle
Limerick - An imposing structure
dramatically situated on the
river. Part of it is being restored
as a museum. Sooner or later the
problem of removing the houses
from within the castle walls
must be met, to allow the full
restoration of the building.

Left - Kanturk Castle Co Cork -
A ruin of architectural and historical importance.

Left - Kenure House, Rush Co
Dublin - A great opportunity was
lost here when this house came
into public ownership. The lands
were developed for housing but
no effort was made to integrate
the house, or its fine landscaping,
into the housing development.

Mistakes like this should not be
repeated.

Hillsborough Co Down and Dun Laoghaire Co Dublin - These town houses from different periods require a policy of preservation. Doors, railings and other elements are all part of an overall concept. To insert larger windows, or remove railings, would effectively destroy their character.

Below - Fitzwilliam Square Dublin Current proposals for the development of several houses in this square should have an influence on the future development of Georgian areas. The existing facades are being retained and restored. Rear gardens are being developed with relatively low buildings, and on the laneway there are to be mews dwellings and flats.

This is a much better approach than the more usual one, of a pastiche type facade hiding a 6/7 storey block behind.

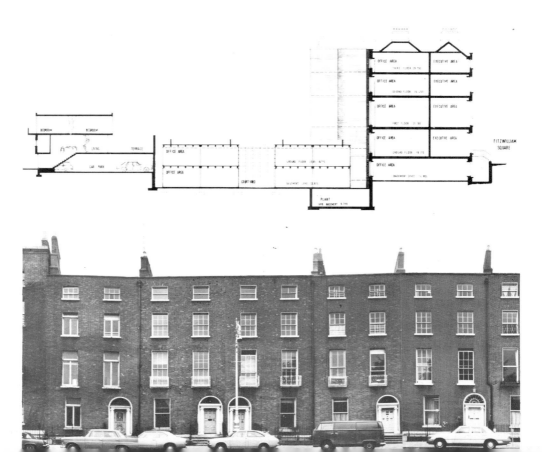

normal ones could be paid. A policy along these lines would give an added impetus to the preservation of buildings in areas of architectural importance.

In most towns there will be other buildings of architectural importance: railway stations, town halls, schools, public and private buildings of many sorts. In most instances they have a distinct architectural expression, are strategically located, and therefore are an important part of the town's architectural heritage. These buildings should be treated with care and understanding. They, too, are also subject to the march of time, to obsolesence, and often suffer from a lack of appreciation and from downright vandalism. There are many opportunities here for re-adaptation and conversion. A number of railway stations have been successfully converted into other uses, particularly the smaller village stations. Others, however, have been mutilated beyond recognition.

This question of new uses for old buildings raises a fundamental issue about conservation in general. In a period of worldwide concern about conservation, existing resources of all kinds must be treated with respect. This should include buildings as well as land, water and air. The demolition of any structurally sound building is a loss of a basic resource, which raises wide conservation and indeed moral problems apart from any aesthetic question. There are many examples of structurally sound buildings being demolished to

Top - The Town Hall Bray Co Wicklow - English in style, but full of character. The standard of detailing and craftsmanship is very high.

Left - Kingscourt Co Cavan - A delightful two storey thatched house and shop in the main street.

Below - Manorhamilton Co Leitrim - This attractive building is the best in the town. It is worthwhile considering a plan for its improvement.

make way for other types of building. This is particularly common in the major cities. The new use is nearly always for offices and sometimes this function could have been carried out just as efficiently in the older buildings. There are examples of old churches being replaced by new churches when perhaps with a little care and imagination, the older church could have been reconstructed. The problems involved in re-adaptation and converting existing buildings must now be given much greater consideration by architects, developers and public bodies. It will not be an easy task. The art of successful conversion will demand new techniques combined with skill and imagination.

OTHER BUILDINGS OF INTEREST

A more complex and difficult matter are those buildings which may not be of intrinsic architectural importance, but because of their location are of fundamental significance to the character of the town. These are the buildings on corners, at the ends of streets, closing off vistas, buildings which form a square or street, or an important space in the town. Their individual architectural quality may not be high, and to the general public they may not appear any different from their neighbours. However, the destruction of such buildings, or insensitive changes in them, can destroy for ever the quality of a local townscape.

Buildings on corners often have a gentle curve which carries one street into the next, emphasising the relationship between the two. This is an art which appears to be lost to modern architecture notwithstanding the flexibility of materials such as concrete. Buildings at the end of a street may create a space or act as a focal point in the street. It may be a simple terrace of good quality houses or a row of interesting shop fronts. There may be a narrowing of a street before the creation of a larger space such as a square or a fair green, an effect noticeable in many towns.

There is always a sense of excitement and mystery when a narrow street leads onto a larger space. Widen this street and the atmosphere is gone forever. There are examples of these subtle relationships being changed to make way for traffic or other modern developments. In the process certain tangible assets have been lost, unnecessary setbacks are provided which may interrupt the profile of the street, gently rounded corners have given way to sharp angled ones to provide sight lines for motorists whose vision anyway is disrupted by pedestrians, parked cars, and by traffic signs. Removing or destroying the relationships of buildings in a square may forever end the sense of enclosure which this square had. The feeling of enclosure is heightened where there are occasional glimpses into the country beyond.

Every town or village in the country has buildings in this category. Many of course even in the smaller towns are worthy of preservation in themselves, but up to now present policies appear to be solely concerned with medieval castles and georgian houses. It is rare to find in a local development plan any reference to shop fronts, a terrace of small houses or indeed to the overall architectural quality of the town. This is a weakness in the 1963 Planning and Development Act. Although it makes provision for the listing of buildings of importance and also for the conservation of areas of natural beauty, the Act

Above - Ardara Co Donegal - buildings like this are worthy of improvement, not because of any great importance in themselves, but because of the atmosphere which they create.

The bend in the street, and the informal appearance of the houses frame an exciting view of the hills beyond. This is what the character of towns is all about, whether in Co Donegal, or in an Italian hill town.

Coleraine Co Derry - These three photographs emphasise the importance of corner buildings to the character of a town. Any insensitive changes to them would damage the qualify and atmosphere of the square.

Left - Baltinglass Co Wicklow - This damaged building is located in an important position in the town. It provides an interesting variation in the street profile and defines the bridge. It is fundamental to the architectural character of the street, and should be reconstructed along its original lines.

makes no provision for declaring conservation areas in towns or villages which are important not from the architectural quality of the individual buildings, but because of the overall effect created by the relationship of the buildings and streets to each other, the materials used, the scale, proportion and landscaping.

The Planning Order 1972 (Northern Ireland) recognises this problem and under this legislation architectural conservation areas can be declared. This will allow special development control procedures to be adopted which will ensure that developments conform with the character of the area. Dublin could follow Belfast's lead with profit in this regard.

However even if the legislation were improved it would not be practicable or even desirable to make every town in the country a conservation area. It would also not be possible to preserve all the buildings which are important from a townscape point of view. The legal and administrative difficulties would be great, and indeed it is not necessary to do so. Many buildings in important positions may be beyond the stage of preservation or even restoration.

However their importance to the overall townscape should be clearly understood, and emphasised in the local development plans. A visual appraisal of any town will bring out and emphasise the important qualities of such buildings. If for any reasons changes have to be made, or buildings replaced, it is vital such changes will not be detrimental to the architectural quality of the town. The plan form, general structure of the building, the materials used, scale and proportion, are qualities that must be respected when changes are made.

This point raises the question of modern architecture and its role in improving the architectural quality of a town. As mentioned before towns are not museum pieces, they are continually changing. Economic and social developments create demands for new buildings of many sorts, schools, offices, shops, churches. These are often built by state and public bodies who have inherited a tradition for high quality civic architecture. A close look at any town will emphasise this. It is important that this tradition is continued in the coming decades.

Notwithstanding any future emphasis on conservation or preservation, it is reasonable to expect that the great mass of developments in towns will be new buildings and therefore modern architecture of some quality or other. To date modern architecture does not appear to have lived up to its traditions. The number of new buildings which are truly modern in concept and design but still reflect the character and style of the town are few indeed. Why is this so? Partly, it is due to unimaginative planning policies which have a deadening effect on design rather than giving a positive lead. Also partly to a lack of understanding on the part of many architects and designers of the constraints which apply when a new building is being erected within the older parts of the town, as opposed to a more open site on the outskirts.

Where architects develop house styles to suit themselves, it is rarely successful to superimpose such styles on their buildings, irrespective of whether they are located in the suburbs, or in a sensitive area of the town with a high architectural quality.

Public bodies should be setting higher standards for their own buildings either through architectural competitions, or by a more sensitive selection of architects and the preparation of briefs for them. Throughout Europe it is

Left - Cobh Co Cork - A highly distinctive way of rounding a corner, note the lovely roof and finely designed steps.

Above - Edenderry Co Offaly - The primary blame here must lie with the Local Authority. There seems little reason for not continuing the existing pitched roof. What a difference it would have made!

Left - Kingscourt Co Cavan - Warehouses similar to this are to be found in many towns. They bring texture and variety to the street and are worth retaining. They could be converted into flats, small offices, or shops.

117

Examples of modern buildings which make little attempt to relate to their surroundings.

5. Department Store, Omagh Co Tyrone.

6. Office Block, Dublin.

7. Hotel Clifden Co Galway

We illustrate four modern buildings where the architects have tackled the problem of knitting the new buildings into the existing streetscapes.

1. Burlington Road Dublin - Although the buildings differ in design, the retention of the trees, and the high qualify of the ground landscaping create a pleasant overall appearance.

2. Office Block Waterford City - The vertical proportions respect the character of the surrounding buildings. The building itself is carried around the corner in a simple and straightforward manner.

3. Omagh Co Tyrone - The new Post Office relates to its surroundings. However, a more varied roof treatment would have resulted in a really good example of modern architecture.

4. Armagh City - This modern building relates satisfactorily both in scale and materials to its Georgian neighbours.

118

Above - A fine old Bank Building, Longford Town.

Left - Examples of Modern Bank Buildings - The old tradition of quality civic architecture has been lost.

Right - Two examples of New Bank Buildings which although modest make some attempt to intigrate with the street.

Above - Portlaoise Town - This new church, although located in an important position, does not help the character of the town.

Milford Co Donegal - a modern church where the scale and materials respect the local architecture.

common practice to have architectural competition for major public projects, and indeed for many minor ones.

There is no guarantee however that architectural competitions will themselves produce great buildings but by and large the particular project is likely to be much more intensively considered and with a good brief could produce imaginative and sensitive buildings.

Competitions would also allow young and talented designers an opportunity to make a name for themselves. The number of architectural competitions held in Ireland are few. Since 1960 the only open competitions for actual projects were for University College Dublin; E.S.B. Headquarters, Fitzwilliam Street Dublin; Trinity College Library Dublin; Ulster Museum Belfast, and more recently a new Post Office in Tipperary town.

The decline in standards of modern architecture can be seen quite clearly in the case of churches and banks. Since. the war there have been many modern churches built in Irish towns. Unfortunately few have contributed to the character of these towns. Indeed when seen in contrast to the older and more dignified churches they compare quite unfavourably. Sometimes it is an alien architectural style inserted into a town and with materials quite foreign to the neighbourhood. The church itself may be totally out of scale and proportion compared to the adjacent buildings. With the present trend towards smaller churches perhaps architects may be able to recapture the charm and quality of the older churches although with a modern expression.

The banks also have inherited a proud tradition of civic architecture. Inspect any town, and invariably among the more imposing and pleasant buildings will be the local bank houses. They were designed in sympathy with their surroundings both as regards materials and architectural style, and located in strategic positions as befitted their economic importance and status. They are examples of civic architecture at its best, and many are worthy of preservation. However, to judge by recent examples of modern bank building this tradition has been lost or forgotten. Far too many new bank buildings appear to have been designed with little reference to the immediate surroundings. Alien materials, the wrong scale,and an insensitive elevation make a sorry contrast with their more distinguished predecessors. Perhaps they reflect modern design standards, and are a taste of what may happen in the future. If so, a fresh approach to urban design is urgently needed.

chapter 10

The Fabric of Towns

MATERIALS

The fabric of a town includes the materials used in the buildings whether it is stone, brick, plaster; the manner in which they are used, the architectural details, such as doors, windows, porches, cornices and various construction details; the small incidental spaces formed by the buildings and the materials with which these spaces are laid out, boundary walls, footpaths. There are also objects distinctive to a particular town; a bridge, a well, a shrine, or a monument erected by past generations in honour of some person or deed.

The fabric, therefore, is made up of elements which in themselves may be quite small but taken together are quite important in determining the character of a town. It is a common sight to see stone or brick bridges and walls being repaired with concrete. Such crude repairs particularly in regard to bridges is surely an offence to a great generation of builders and engineers, their work should be respected.

Windows are inserted into buildings which radically change their character, unique and distinctive lettering is removed from shop fronts, and replaced by tasteless and commonplace plastic lettering. Stone paved footpaths are replaced by crudely laid tarmacadam. There are also examples of coloured brick, or imitation stone fronts being inserted into a street of plaster and painted houses. The reverse is equally discordant. Multi-colour roof tiles, used where all the other roofs are of slates or dark grey tiles. Or worse still a flat roof structure in a street where the other roofs are pitched.

Such things happen, however, as a result of natural and evolutionary changes and are a fact of life. A stone wall may have been damaged by traffic, buildings are constantly in need of repair, windows and roofs need replacement. It is quite feasible however to accommodate such changes without affecting the quality of the town, or putting unnecessary expense on to the property owner. Certain settlements, particularly the small estate villages, may have a common design theme. This may derive from a common use of stone or brick for buildings, boundary walls, and other details. Although it is rarely possible nowadays to erect new buildings in stone, the general texture and overall colour can be matched by careful use of materials which are not unduly expensive.

Architectural Details - Here we illustrate examples
of local craftsmanship and building techniques
They are important visually and architecturally
and should be looked after with
care and understanding.

It should be possible to incorporate local buildings
traditions and materials into new developments.

A detail common to many towns, particularly the market towns, is the archway leading in to the long rear gardens. The use of this particular detail adds interest to the shopping street. Almost always it is built over and thereby links one building to another. This, of course, is one of the principal reasons why many streets have such unity of expression despite the various types of buildings in it. Sometimes the arches are executed in stone and strongly modelled but usually they are more simple in expression and plastered over to match the adjacent buildings.

Such details should not be lost in any redevelopments and indeed they could form appropriate and interesting entrances to new developments which may be carried out in the back areas, many of which are in urgent need of redevelopment. It is only by making the general public aware of the importance of the building and architectural deatils that they will be appreciated and stand a better chance of being protected. This is an aspect of urban conservation which appears to be eminently suitable for school projects. It should be possible as part of the geography or civics class to request the school children to make a survey of all the small details which are to be found in every town. One approach to this is discussed in Page 177

SHOPFRONTS

One of the features of Irish vernacular architecture is the quality and design of the traditional shopfronts. They can be seen everywhere in the country. Nearly every town or small village has at least one example. They come in all shapes and sizes, ranging from the highly ornamental and ornate facades with details from many periods and styles of architecture, to the smaller shop with a simple but dignified expression of its function, and with the owner's name displayed in clear but bold lettering. There is a grandeur and vigour about the designs generally which is not found in many other countries. Certain styles and designs are associated with different types of shops, for example, drapery and clothing shops are generally more elegant with windows divided by slender timber columns and arches; the pub on the other hand, is more sturdily detailed with bold but intricate lettering—a more robust approach to a different type business. In the smaller towns the pub might also include a general store selling a variety of goods from hardware to clothes.

The chemist shops, successors of the old apothecaries, often have a distinctive appearance marked by a crisp, clean and shiny front with interesting and elegant signs. In the smaller shops the details are more simple although still constructed in the classical idiom. It may have a simple timber column instead of the more ornate one in polished granite, but the overall design quality is just as high.

Names and signs are important in shop front design, particularly in the smaller towns. They identify a family, with their own style and tradition. Often a family which has been trading in the town for many generations will take particular pride in the sign over their shop front. This is not another branch of the faceless multiple, but a trader whose name is respected, and the service he provides appreciated. Such shopfronts are living examples of local craftsmen, the carpenter, painter and sign writer, working at their best and with materials

124

Above and left - Details like this are part of a town's history. The express a function relating to another age or remember a local dignitary or event.

Below - Many of our bridges are a monument to the work of engineers and craftsmen of the past. They set high standards of design and building techniques. Even if not in use they are still worth preserving.

Below right - This type of insensitive bridge repair is all too common.

The arch is an interesting and attractive architectural device, and a great variety of types can be found throughout the country.

1 and 2 Hillsborough Co Down
3 Blessington Co Wicklow
4 Ballinasloe · Co Galway
5 Kilkenny City.

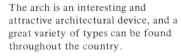

Steps create an atmosphere of myste beckoning the onlooker to visit a sec place or to admire a view. Above al they ensure that the pedestrian has precedence, as the motor car cannot yet climb steps.

1. Youghal Co Cork, 2 Dun Laoghai 3. Drumshambo Co Leitrim.

Doorways are always important, and traditionally great attention has been paid to their design. A great variety of doorways are to be found throughout the country, and they range from the small but effective cottage types to the ornate and impressive designs that adorn the entrances to the larger town houses.

Below - Developments which show lack of attention to detail.

Left - Reconstruction of a house. The windows are out of proportion and the stone facade appears to have been plastered over.

Right - The break in the roof, the horizontal proportion of the windows and the choice of materials are all details of this new shop which are out of keeping with the street.

they understood and cared for. Unfortunately in the last few years there are many instances of fine shopfronts being either removed completely, or destroyed beyond recognition in the interest of modernisation. Dignified fascias have been ripped out and replaced with crude timber sheeting, vulgar plastic names and signs. The whole traditional art of sign writing is in danger of disappearing completely.

In other cases entire shopfronts are being removed and replaced by modern facades. These rarely display any real design sense and are often insensitive to the character of the town. This is happening all over the country in large towns and small villages. There are streets where nearly all the facades have been destroyed or disfigured. It appears to be the new type of typically modern shop, for example the multiple firm, supermarket, the lounge bar, that are the worst offenders. In this mad rush of modernisation many fine interiors, particularly in pubs, have also been destroyed or altered. Some have been of extremely high quality both in design and craftsmanship, and worthy of preservation. There is now a distinct possibility that one of the great features of Irish architecture will be lost forever and replaced by an ubiquitous and mediocre style of architecture which can be seen in any town or city in the Western world.

This is not a plea for complete preservation at all costs, but rather it is a criticism against the standards of the new architecture which, except for a few isolated examples, have not in any way matched up to the great qualities of their predecessors. Shops do change hands, and their function also changes. The shop interior and the buidling itself may be in poor condition requiring a complete new redevelopment, but it is a pity that in one of the areas where we have a tradition of high design standards the modern shopfronts

This is not a plea for complete preservation at all costs, but rather it is a criticism against the standards of the new architecture which, except for a few isolated examples, have not in any way matched up to the great qualities of their predecessors. Shops do change hands, and their function also changes. The shop interior and the building itself may be in poor condition requiring a complete new redevelopment, but it is a pity that in one of the areas where we have a tradition of high design standards that the modern shopfronts should be so disappointing.

The concept and spread of the multiple shop with its universal expression as regards function, service, and architecture does not help matters. It seeks to impose its image by providing the same range of services all over the country. It aims to have the same architectural expression irrespective of the quality, character, and scale of the town or street into which it is inserted. Sales and market research organisations will say that people react to certain styles of architecture, and that every multiple should develop their own distinctive design. But surely it is not beyond the wit of architects and designers to give the multiple firm a certain identity while at the same time accepting the general design constraints imposed by the street or town. If the bigger firms cannot be made to respect the local architecture, then it is more difficult to ask the smaller man, anxious to modernise his shopfront, to do so.

Here is a major aesthetic problem involving architectural conservation. Although there is legislation under the planning act to ensure that there are

Shop Fronts - In the towns and villages throughout the country simple and attractive shopfronts are to be found. They add style and individuality to a street and are an important part of our heritage.

If we continue with our remorseless destruction of these fine examples of Irish craftsmanship, we may stand indicted by future generations for sheer vandalism.

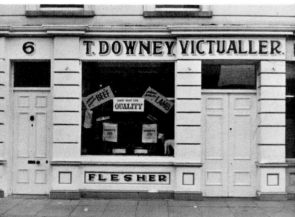

proper standards of design, experience to date indicates that it is extremely difficult, if not impossible, to legislate for good taste. But, even so, it should still be possible to conserve, in a realistic way, many of the remaining traditional shopfronts. In many towns there are really outstanding examples which should be preserved at all costs, and are as worthy of preservation as a church, castle or Georgian house.

Right - Mullingar Co Westmeath - The use of a signwriter would have solved the problem created by the change of ownership, without taking away from the character of this shop front, one of the best in the town.

Left - Also in Mullingar - Two contrasting shop fronts. The one on the right a modern one restored to its original appearance, and it has not suffered from a business point of view.

Below - It is quite possible for similar improvements to be carried out to the other shop as shown in the sketch.

Modern Shop Fronts - What a sad reflection on present day standards, no attempt has been made to blend the new shop into the streetscape. The brash and insensitive use of plastic, tiles and mosaic is commonplace. Quite often when one new shopfront appears in a town others quickly follow, and soon the character of place is submerged.

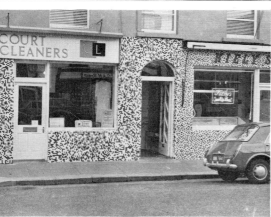

Irish towns have established a great tradition in the use of strong bright colours. The black and white colouring of this group of buildings in Roundwood Co Wicklow is very effective. It is also a more economical way of presenting buildings rather than by using a variety of materials.

COLOUR

There is a tradition in Ireland for strong and bright colours which can be seen not only in the towns but throughout the countryside as well. This use of strong colours together with the generally spacious layout creates an atmosphere of lightness and gaiety. This traditional use of strong colour should be continued and given every encouragement by local planning authorities and community associations. It gives our towns a distinctive and unique appearance, different from towns in Britain and Europe, The colour harmony may not be of textbook standards but it is all the better for this.

The effect of Bord Failte's Tidy Town's Competition has given a new impetus to this tradition. There is a section dealing with colour and colour harmony, and special prizes are awarded. Towns which were drab and dull have now become bright and colourful. In some instances local committees have retained colour consultants to advise. This concern and interest deserved credit, but there can be dangers in such co-ordinated schemes. They can and do look contrived, especially if the consultant is too specific in his recommendations and adheres too closely to textbook ideas. Better to give the local committee a range of colours and allow each property owner select his own. He may have many reasons for it. He may wish to assert his own importance, individuality and character. As a general rule, especially in areas of diverse architectural styles such as shopping streets, the general use of white for windows and reveals helps to relieve and relate the strongest and most contrasting colours. The use of strong colour on strategically located buildings at corners or ends of streets will help considerably in adding to the character of a town. When dealing with groups of buildings with a more unified expression a more formal painting scheme may be necessary to reflect the architecture.

STREET FURNITURE

The modern town contains a multitude of items commonly called street furniture. This consists of advertisements, electricity and telegraph poles, wires, traffic signs, road markings and a variety of other details. There is perhaps more need for them because of the complexities of modern life, but as a general rule they do little except introduce an appearance of chaos and disorder to the average street scene. Even the smallest villages now have their neon signs and national advertisements.

The problem is not however the concept of street furniture, but its general design and location in towns and villages. Towns are not museums and there is a genuine need for traders to advertise their wares and services. There is also a

132

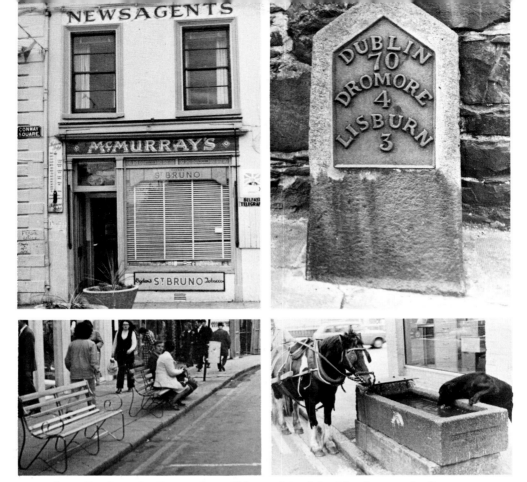

Street Furniture - In all towns there will be a variety of street furniture, ranging from signwriting to more esoteric objects which now have perhaps only a historical significance. If well presented and maintained they will add to the character and appearance of a town.

necessity to control and direct traffic. The public service companies have a duty to provide public utilities of all types. The need for such services varies from town to town, but the overall demand is increasing from year to year. However, it should be possible for street furniture to be arranged in an organised and tidy fashion while at the same time fulfilling its particular function. It therefore can bring a sense of uniformity and order into a town rather than disorder, carelessness and untidiness.

ADVERTISEMENTS

In discussing street furniture, advertising signs immediately spring to mind. These signs are being erected indiscriminately not only in the busy shopping streets (where perhaps they are more logically located) but in the small scale setting of a village where a single large sign can destroy its visual character. Advertisements are part of modern commercial life, and it can be argued that many shopping streets would be dull places if all advertisements were to be banned. On the other hand, however, it is difficult to accept that there is an absolute necessity for so much advertising in the average street, especially the

133

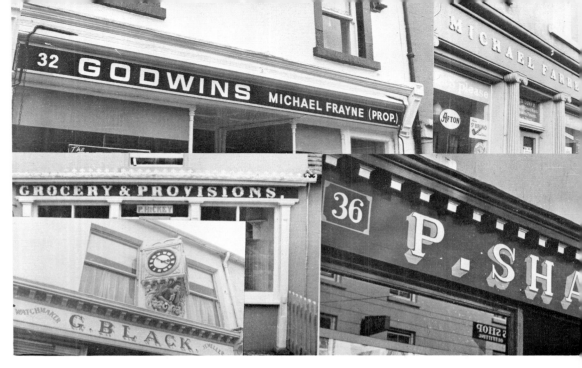

In Irish towns names are still important. Long may this continue.

cumbersome neon signs projecting out from the wall which can destroy the visual character of the facade and at the same time put an unnecessary physical strain on the building. It is not uncommon to see four or five different types of advertisements attached to the one premises. Some traders must feel that they will lose out if their name is not displayed two or three times. It would appear as if the sole objective in many towns is to cover the main shopping street with as many advertisements and other paraphenalia as possible. Indeed in some streets it is impossible to distinguish the facades from the signs, and in the grand confusion it is difficult to receive any message.

The amalgamation of the major banks has also resulted in a rash of modern signs disfiguring many fine buildings. Certain banks have now three or four signs indicating their presence, as if one would visit the bank on impulse the same as a pub or grocer. The need for uniformity and identity is appreciated. This could have been achieved by a smaller sign set in the windows. To erect the larger signs on the facades of buildings irrespective of the architecture or scale is an affront to good taste.

Often the worst offenders are the large nationwide companies, many of whom seem to be solely concerned with selling their image and products irrespective of any environmental consequences. The major advertising companies must also share the blame. They seek out the most advantageous position to erect their hoardings—on gable walls, at the entrances to towns, or adjacent to important buildings in the main squares. Occasionally they may fit in well with the overall environment, but this appears to be a hit and miss matter rather than from any thoughtful consideration.

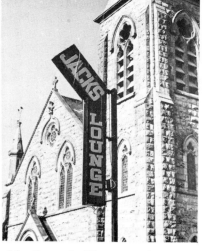

Advertisements - The use or misuse of advertising signs often damages the appearance of a building.

Left - Two contrasting approaches to advertisements in Ballinasloe Co Galway. Both buildings are cinemas and are in use. One displays a large advertisement sign which is totally out of place with the building. The other cinema functions quite well without a large sign. Perhaps there is a message here.

Left - Athlone Co Westmeath - The large neon signs can be inappropriate both by day and night. We must now question the need for such signs on energy grounds alone.

Below - Bank Signs - The banks had once a fine tradition in signwriting. In years gone by the names were designed to fit in with the architecture of the building. The amalgamation of the banks brought the end of this. Now a standard type of sign is put on a bank, irrespective of its scale or architecture. This policy should be altered.

The situation is somewhat ludicrous when you consider that current planning legislation covers advertisements. The Planning Act includes sections devoted entirely to this problem. In principle all advertisements over a certain size require planning permission. Most urban development plans contain a section dealing with advertisement, and have specific policies relating to their design and siting. There is an obvious gap between the policies and objectives of local authorities, and the actual realities on the ground. Perhaps without planning legislation the situation may have been immeasurably worse. There should be stronger attempts by local authorities to control the spread and type of advertisements. It is not enough to say in the development plan that advertisements must be of good design and sympathetic in scale. This means nothing, and of course can create a situation where all sorts of advertisements are allowed. It it not a difficult problem. At the present time most advertisers have only a temporary planning permission, and it should be possible over a period of say three years for local authorities to remove the most offensive ones and to identify areas where advertising can be allowed, also to suggest a specific design and standard relating to particular locations. To property owners a 'national type advertisement' is a small source of revenue. But surely this is not a reason to allow some of the more offensive ones to remain. They would hardly be in financial difficulty if the advertisement signs were removed. The companies might lose much more.

The Department of Local Government in Dublin have published a booklet drawing attention to the problems of street advertising and the need for a creative approach. This appears to have been completely ignored by local planning authorities. The time is ripe to tackle the problem again.

WIRESCAPE

The rather grim word commonly given to the proliferation of telegraph and electricity poles and overhead wires of all sorts is wirescape. The problem of wirescape is a feature of modern society, and is a direct result of the demand for public utility services, lighting, power, telecommunication. It is an unfortunate visual feature in many towns. Until recently it was considered expensive and uneconomic to lay such services under ground. This was the case both in the new housing areas, and in the shopping streets. The sole objective was to provide the service, little consideration was given to whether a pole would obstruct the view of a building or take away from it in any way.

In recent years there has been a welcome change in policy. All services in new development areas are being put underground. The improvement in techniques and a welcome public conern for the visual appearance of the new housing estates have created this situation. There still remains the problem of dealing with the older areas, where wires and poles of many kinds cut across vistas and obliterate views of buildings, and generally take away from the appearance of towns.

The intensity of street lighting is now being increased, but the methods adopted do not improve the appearance of towns. It is a common sight to see the new street lighting fixed on top of existing timber poles with an obvious lack of any concern for the visual effect.

There is really no need for advertising signs to be out of scale with the building. All these signs relate to the function of the business, and respect the architecture instead of destroying it.

Top Left - Trim Co Meath

Top Right - Dromore Co Down

Centre left - Parkgate Street Dublin

Centre right - Near Ballycotton Co Cork

Bottom - Crawfordsburn Co Down

The problem of unsightly street furniture is common to all countries. If any local authority or local voluntary organisation were to take even a small section of a town and remove the wires and poles, certain advertisements, and general clutter, the result would be a tremendous improvement. Poles might be sited in more discreet locations, for example, to the rear of premises rather than at the front. Wires could be parallel to the buildings instead of directly crossing the street 'willy nilly' as they do in many cases.

The light fittings could be fixed to the buildings and the wires carried along under the eaves. Mounting the lamps on buildings instead of poles would appear to be more economic, although it may cause some administrative difficulties. The standard of lighting can also be related to the particular settlement depending on its size. There is something incongruous and inconsistent about a small village which is overpowered at night with street lighting. There are many new techniques available which can improve the general situation.

In the North of Ireland many towns have solved the problem to a great extent. The wires and street lamps have been attached to the buildings. Surely this could also be done throughout the country pending major improvements which would enable all services to be put underground. A start has been made in Adare Co Limerick, where wires have been put underground, and the lighting attached to the buildings wherever possible. This should now be extended elsewhere.

Examples of Wirescape -

Left - Bandon Co Cork - Poles and wires of all types are located in towns all over the country without any aesthetic consideration whatsoever. (It was difficult to take many of the photographs for this book. As often as not an ugly pole of some sort was disrupting the shot).

Below - Trim Co Meath - Signs and wires create a sense of confusion rather than clarity.

Adding to the general clutter is the familiar T.V. aerial. A sure reminder that 'Mac Luhan World Village' is already upon us. The move towards piped T.V. will improve matters. One major mast is much less offensive than the myriads of aerials probing into the sky.

ROAD SIGNS

It is a common sight to see a variety of direction signs which confuse the motorist rather than help him. They are often erected with a minimum of concern for visual effect, and indeed sometimes also for guidance. Temporary road signs are also a problem. These may be erected pending a more permanent sign or to give advance notice of road works. Although they are temporary they often have the habit of remaining a year or so. Rusty tar barrels indicating such development are not a very good advertisement for the community or local authority. A standardised approach to road signs, both in the towns and throughout the country as a whole is required. There is a need for road signs of all sorts because of increased traffic and the general mobility of the population. Some guiding principles are necessary.

Road signs have a function, and there is no point in erecting them where they cannot be seen. Wherever possible the number should be reduced. There is no need for two or three signs saying the same thing, especially if they are

Top - A barren landscape, decorated with Television aerials.

Right - Clonmel Co Tipperary - Here the overhead wires are strung parallel to the building, and as a result the appearance is considerably improved. Pending the undergrounding of all services this approach should be adopted.

Good Wirescape - Where services are put underground
the appearance of a town is considerably improved.
Lampstandards can also be fitted to the buildings.

Below - Portaferry and Donaghadee Co Down.

Left - Adare Co Limerick.

located badly. It is important both visually and from a safety viewpoint that
signs are properly maintained. Many are unreadable because of dirt, they are
then more of a hazard than a help. When maintained they add a crisp
appearance to a town.

The design of these signs should be related to the speed at which one is
driving and the particular function of the sign. Within towns and villages
directional signs may be smaller than in the open countryside. The clean white
line running down the centre of a well maintained roadway is a satisfactory
sight in itself, and provides a suitable setting for the architecture of the town.

STREET NAMES

Street names often tell the tale of a town. The very name of a street or area
may indicate an aspect of history long since disappeared. They not only honour
historical figures associated with particular places, but in the older towns are
living evidence of a way of life long since gone. Names such as Butter Market,
Haymarket and Potato Market spring to mind, and the trades and businesses
are represented by names such as Tailor's Row, Fishamble Street, Skippers
Alley, Mariner's Row and Threadneedle Street. Every street name has a history

Above - The newer signs are much better but there is an urgent need for a standardised approach throughout the country.

Right - Road Signs like these apart from being rather crudely positioned are difficult to read.

Below - Trim Co Meath - The lettering on the new nameplates is very good indeed. Other Local Authorities could profit from this example.

of some sort behind it, and often has a special meaning for the local inhabitants. It is worthwhile cherishing them.

The older name places have set high standards of design, and are often works of art, sometimes chiselled out of the stonework from which the buildings were constructed. They are positive reminders of the craftsmanship of past generations. Traditionally they were erected on corner buildings at an approximate height of twelve to fourteen feet. Other signs were executed in cast iron with attractive lettering and mounted onto the building. With redevelopment many such signs have disappeared, often to turn up as curios in antique shops and private homes. There is still a need to identify streets and buildings. The design of signs is something that could be considered of little importance, but it adds to the appearance of an area as well as continuing a fine tradition.

Local authorities should have a clear policy in this respect. They should establish a consistency about the location, height and lettering to be used and ensure that they are durable and easily maintained. In many instances the same fine letting which may have been used in the past can be repeated in the context of a modern sign.

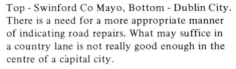

Top - Swinford Co Mayo, Bottom - Dublin City.
There is a need for a more appropriate manner
of indicating road repairs. What may suffice in
a country lane is not really good enough in the
centre of a capital city.

Top - Blackwater Co Wexford, Bottom -
Ballyconnell Co Cavan.
Both towns have been award winners in Bord
Failte's Tidy Towns Competition.

TIDINESS

Perhaps the most important detail which determines the appearance of a town
to the visitor or traveller is its general tidiness and absence of litter. Here is
something that Irish towns cannot be proud of, more particularly in the South.
Notwithstanding the efforts of the 'Tidy Towns Competition', which has
achieved great results, the general appearance of many towns and cities still
leaves a lot to be desired. Streets are often full of litter, there are too many
derelict areas, cars are dumped in conspicuous places and open spaces are left
untidy. This gives the impression of a community unconcerned about its
appearance and too lazy to do anything about it. A massive public relations
campaign, concentrating mainly on the schools, is required to tackle what can
really be called 'a national malaise'.

Tidiness by itself will make a valuable contribution towards improving the
image of a town. Advertisements could be removed, and others more tastefully
displayed. In certain cases the same advertising value might be achieved by sign
writing rather than neon or plastic signs and much cheaper too. Road signs
should be streamlined and more effectively positioned, walls and footpaths
repaired, houses and shop fronts painted, and derelict areas cleaned up and put
to better use.

There is a saying that 'cleanliness is next to Godliness'. This may be open
to different interpretations, but a clean and tidy town is something to be proud
of. There is no virtue in dirt. A town can be old and peaceful but if its streets
are tidy it has dignity. On the other hand, a town may be busy, brash and alive
with activity, but if its streets are litter strewn and dirty there is a shallowness
about its prosperity.

chapter 11

A Policy for Conservation

(1)

THE PUBLIC ROLE

The underlining philosophy of urban conservation is that towns can undergo both social and economic expansion, and physical change, without losing their essential character. The success, therefore, of this policy is dependent on two important factors. Firstly, it must have the general backing of the public, and secondly, there should be a more positive and imaginative policy towards conservation adopted by local planning authorities. The general public have both the political strength and emotional persuasion to ensure that conservation policies are formulated, and legislation improved where necessary. Local authorities have the necessary administrative powers to enforce such policies.

To achieve the first objective is a difficult and complex task. It will not be achieved overnight at the wave of a magic wand or indeed because of the proclamation of 'An Architectural Heritage Year'. Many different approaches will be required; an appeal perhaps to the personal and business instincts in man might be a good start, making the case that conservation is good value for money, and that a conservation policy can mean more money in the till at the end of the day. An appeal to cultural and philosophical instincts emphasising that every society must be concerned to conserve all that is fine in its civilisation whether it is painting, music, literature, works of nature, or the works of man as expressed in the quality of towns and villages.

To make this possible the public should be fully aware of what is involved. They should understand and appreciate the architectural heritage and visual quality of their particular town, fully aware of what makes it different from others. The mistakes that have been made in the past will have to be clearly and simply explained, not specifically to embarrass individuals, but to avoid similar mistakes in the future. There are many ways that this can be done depending on the size of the town, and it will need the enthusiasm and commitment of both the local planning, and local education authorities, and of course the general interest of the public.

Public appreciation about architecture, and the visual arts generally, is not a strong feature of Irish life. Take up any book, pamphlet or tourist guide about towns; it is mainly concerned with historical and political activities, and

Page 143 - Public in action - a group of voluntary workers in Edenderry
and the start of an An Taisce walk through Dublin.

This is a conservation project. The seven project members have all an interest in conservation. The area we intend to conserve includes Shop Street Bridge and its environs. We chose this area because some months ago it was seriously suggested that the bridge be removed, the river covered and the site cleared in order to make space for a much sought car park. We feel that if such a plan were carried out it would rob the town of the character which the bridge and the river give it and that the most historical site in Tuam would be covered forever with tar and cement. We feel also that this suggestion would not solve the parking problem and that the covering of the area with tarmacadam would be very uneconomical. We intend to suggest two alternative sites for the car park, both of which we feel would be more economical and more serviceable as car parks.

We will in the course of this project draw up a plan for the redevelopment of the site and the highlighting of the historical features situated both on and near it. This plan will be illustrated by maps, sketches and a model of the whole area as we feel it should be developed.

Michael Flaherty (captain) John Loftus   Damien McGrath

Liam Kelly   Frederick McDonogh Sean Moggan

John O'Gorman

Tuam Co Galway - The old mill and environs have been saved through the efforts of a dedicated band of young people. The mill is now open as a museum and the wheel is restored and in operation.

it is a rare thing indeed to find any significant reference to architectural and aesthetic qualities. In recent years there have been discussions and controversy about the environment and the decline in environmental standards. There has been public concern about natural resources, the pollution of the coast, lakes and rivers, and the general appearance of the countryside. Apart from the large cities (and a few isolated cases in towns) there has been little discussion about architectural problems. The reason of course is simple. The architectural and townscape qualities of towns are not nearly as well known and appreciated as they should be. Most people are unaware of its particular plan and layout; have little knowledge or appreciation of any but the most important buildings, and sometimes not even these. They may be completely ignorant of the fine craftsmanship, and perhaps unique use of materials which may be found in our towns.

As with other major problems of to-day, a commitment by young people is important. The same point has been repeated so often in regard to other issues that it is now something of a cliche. Nevertheless it is still true. In the natural sequence of events the youth of to-day are the decision makers of tomorrow. The decisions which affect the environment are man made and influenced by personal and political factors. It is particularly important therefore to involve young people in planning and architectural matters, and instill in them an appreciation of the architectural heritage of their community. If society is concerned, and rightly so, about natural and biological pollution it should also be concerned about visual pollution.

Fortunately it is a subject open to imaginative educational methods. It is now an opportune time for activities of this sort. The improvement in living standards has resulted in a more comprehensive approach to education. It is no longer a matter of achieving minimum standards in reading, writing and arithmetic, with the sole aim of passing examinations, although the examination neurosis still heavily influences the teaching of many subjects. There is a whole range of activities that can be designed to stimulate the interest of young people in the architecture of their own neighbourhood. Education can be taken out of the classroom and into the local environment, and the techniques used

145

in schools can also be used for adult education, and for informing the public at large.

More emphasis should be given to architecture, town planning and conservation in the civic and environmental courses now being operated in primary and secondary levels. It is just as important for young people to appreciate visual beauty as well as literature and history. Architectural appreciation, and design generally, should be considered as suitable subjects for university entrance. At present environmental education is an optional subject at secondary level, and as it is not generally included as an examination subject it is often forgotten about. In other countries there is more recognition of design education and architectural appreciation. Certain examination boards in Britain are now providing the 'A' Level courses in these subjects.

The local town or village itself provides the classroom and back-up facilities. The town is a laboratory made up of many aspects all gathered together for everyone to see. It is readily available, costs nothing ot use, its elements are constantly changing due to the pressures of modern life. It reflects the lives and times of generations past, of notable people and of the more humble, but no less important, whose contribution can be equally observed. Children will be studying their own roots, and it is as necessary for a young person to know and understand his own local environment as it is to learn statistics and facts about faraway places. It is a reflection on education generally when children know little about the history and life of their own town. This, unfortunately, is a common situation.

COMPETITIONS AND PROJECTS

One way of stimulating interest in local architecture is by means of competitions and projects. The value of this approach is now widely appreciated. Competitions could be used to identify and list the architecture of the local town, to recognise the threats to its character from such problems as traffic and new developments, to bring home the need to preserve old buildings. This method can lead to the discovery of new uses for buildings which may be functionally obsolete, but still have a long life from a physical point of view, and are important to the character of the town. Local organisations and firms could sponsor such competitions. A visit to the more remarkable architectural places in Ireland or Europe might be awarded as prizes.

Think of the interest that could be stimulated if the local schools were asked to suggest ways and means of saving and restoring an old warehouse or church, of listing and identifying the various types of trees growing in their town, of using the excellent lettering still to be found on many shop fronts as a means of stimulating interest in graphic art and design generally. The schoolchild will learn more about life generally through exercises of this sort than relying solely on some textbook, the relevance of which they do not fully understand. There is an old teaching adage which says "I hear and I forget, I see and I remember, I do and I understand". This is very true in the field of design education.

There are now some encouraging signs in this direction An Taisce, the

American Embassy Dublin.

Above - An Taisce - The National Trust for Ireland has made awards for outstanding projects in the field of urban conservation. Among the winners were The Market House in Kildare, (page 107), a Georgian building at South Leinster Street Dublin that was restored following representation by the Dublin Civic Group, and the American Embassy Dublin.

Right - Damer House Roscrea Co Tipperary - The County Council had intended to demolish this building and use the site as a car park. However, in response to local pressures it was leased to the Irish Georgian Society for 99 years. The Society, with the help of the Old Roscrea Society, is restoring the house as its project for European Architectural Heritage Year 1975. It is intended that the house will become a local museum and cultural centre.

Right - The Ulster Architectural Heritage Society has in their surveys drawn attention to the groups of ordinary buildings which contribute to the quality of so many Ulster towns, and also to the bad examples of modern architecture which are destroying the character of towns.
The two examples from Killyleagh Co Down illustrate these points.
"This was once a dignified if narrow street of late-Georgian houses and stone warehouses running uphill to the turrets of the Castle."

Below - "An extremely fine three-storey Georgian house, very well painted and cared for. The upper floors are of five bays, with a crenellated string-course dividing the small windows under the eaves from the large ones below. The ground floor is rusticated, with one very large window on either side of the central doorcase; all three have heavy mouldings with keystones: the rectangular doorcase contains an attractive cobweb fanlight."

National Trust for Ireland, organised an architectural competition for post primary schools along these lines as a part of their contribution to European Architectural Heritage Year. It attracted an entry of over three hundred. This is a welcome move.

Perhaps the most interesting possibility as regards education at both youth and adult level is the concept of the town trail. Over the past decade or so the concept of Nature Trails has been developed in many countries. This is a device designed to stimulate in people an understanding and appreciation of nature by experiencing it at first hand. Following European Conservation Year in 1970, Nature Trails of various sorts were established in Ireland and throughout Europe. Town trails have originated from this concept. The town trail is different from the nature trail. It takes the form of a walk through a town or village starting off from an important vantage point from where the whole town can be observed. The top of a building or a nearby hill are suitable starting points, and ending at a similar focal point, such as town square, a public building or open space. The intention would be to observe and appraise all the important elements in the town. This would include areas of architectural importance, the main shopping streets, the residential areas, open spaces, the landscaping; in fact all the elements mentioned previously in this book. Participants would record the individual buildings, their architectural character, present appearance, the facts and statistics about their history, the various activities that took place in them, and the people involved in such activities. Identifying the problems now facing the town whether it is traffic, the poor quality of new design, or the controversy being aroused by a particular proposal could feature in the trail.

Those taking part are asked to make their own observations as to why they like one particular building or area and not another, making their comments and observations by means of notes, sketches, photographs. The town trail could form part of a school programme, adult education course or community activity. The results can be processed and analysed for discussion and debate. Indeed participants are likely to see their town or city properly for the first time, and will probably be surprised at what they discover for themselves.

The town trail is quite different to the guided tour, which has been the traditional way of viewing towns and cities. In the town trail the leader would give a short introduction, suggest possible techniques, and provide a check list of what might be looked at. The rest is up to the participant. The whole emphasis is on participation, a do-it-yourself approach to getting to know the local architectural heritage rather than being told about it.

Page 179 includes a general outline of what could be covered by a town trail. Each town requires its own individual approach.

PLANNERS AND ARCHITECTS

Architects and town planners should be prepared to take the lead. They, above all others, have a special interest in ensuring that public opinion is adequately informed as regards architecture generally. A wider public understanding and appreciation of architecture is a prerequisite for higher standards.

Above - Seaforde Co Down - 'Hearth'
Housing Association purchased sixteen
buildings including almshouses, a courthouse,
a blacksmith's shop and store. These are
now being converted into thirteen separate
dwellings. The scheme will make a significant
contribution to retaining the architectural
character of the village while at the same
time achieving a worthwhile social objective.

Left - Drumaness Co Down - The Ulster
Architectural Heritage Society in their
booklet on Mid-Down have drawn attention
to the quality and character of this old
mill village. In particular they emphasised
the attractive local tradition of using
random stone with brick dressings.

It is no longer only individuals with money and power who commission
architects. Everyone may do so from the person who is building a single house
to the public committee commissioning a school or large housing project.
Architects should also be prepared to talk to local groups about their buildings
and projects. Urban study centres could be organised in co-operation with the
local education committee and voluntary organisations. These would be
particularly valuable in the larger towns where photographs and plans of the
major developments could be exhibited and then discussed with the local
people by the architects and developers involved.

Of the professions involved in architectural conservation, architects and
town planners have the greatest responsibility. They are, or should be, the front
line soldiers who lead the fight to protect the buildings and areas which are
worthy of protection and ensure that the new buildings and developments are

in sympathy with their surroundings. It is the planners and architects who shape the environment that will last for many generations. They translate into physical terms decisions made by politicans, developers and the general public. They have a responsibility to society at large, and to future generations, just as they have a responsibility to their client. In certain instances there may be a conflict between the aims of an architect's client and the aims of the community. As professionals, and inheritors of a fine tradition for civic design, they must try to reduce such conflicts. To opt out of this and consider that their responsibility is solely to their client and let others, the conservationists, take care of the community aims, could in the long run affect the image and standing of the profession.

There are signs that this is already happening both in Ireland, and in other countries. Many people are concerned about the quality of modern developments, their inhumanity, standardisation, lack of respect for human values and human scale. They consider that they have been designed by architects for developers purely in response to economic requirements. They compare them with the work of previous generations, often not designed by architects, and they are found wanting. This is a grave situation and suggests a new approach to architecture by architects themselves.

On the other hand architects have been subject to tremendous pressures to obtain the maximum financial return irrespective of architectural or design considerations. Indeed it is hard to escape the conclusion that in many instances major office developments are influenced more by the estate agent than by the architect. If, as now seems likely, there is to be a slow down in the demand for office developments and also in the wholesale demolition of structurally sound properties, perhaps architects will be able to reassert their importance as a profession.

The Schools of Architecture and Planning in Queen's University, Belfast; University College Dublin; and the College of Technology Dublin, have over the past few years undertaken many interesting studies of towns and villages in Ireland. These studies which are an important part of the educational process for architects and planners, have been carried out in co-operation with local organisations. They are extremely thorough and comprehensive and have been of considerable help to local organisations.

VOLUNTARY BODIES

There are a number of organisations active in the field of architectural conservation which is a good omen for the future and suggests that there is a hard core of opinion on which a more enlightened public attitude could be built. An Taisce, the National Trust of Ireland, founded in 1948, has now over 7,000 members with twenty-six local associations throughout the country. Its members are concerned about conservation issues of all kinds, but An Taisce has a particularly good reputation as regards architectural conservation. The Amenity Study of Dun Laoghaire and Dublin published in 1967 greatly influenced the subsequent re-development of the city. This comprehensive report, produced voluntarily by a dedicated and skilled band of professional and lay people, did more than any other document in recent years in drawing

Left - Tyrrellspass Co Westmeath - Before and after its success in the Tidy Town's Competition.

Below - Malin Co Donegal - The village green at the turn of the century. The green is now one of the best in the country. (see page 61) This is due principally to the enthusiastic involvement of the local community in the Tidy Town's Competition, and perhaps saved the green from becoming perhaps a dump, or a parking lot, which is the case in many other villages.

Left - Ballyconnell Co Cavan - One of the successes of the Tidy Town's Competition has been the impetus given to tree planting within towns. The main street of this town has been considerably improved by recent tree planting.

public attention to the importance of Dublin's architectural heritage. It emphasised not only the importance of individual buildings but the streets and spaces, and squares formed by these buildings. It is a fine example of what can be achieved by voluntary associations. An Taisce is also publishing architectural guides to a number of towns. These booklets will highlight the architectural qualities of the town as well as drawing attention to the various problems which they have. This indeed is a welcome innovation because as a general rule guide books are concerned only with historical data and tourist facilities. It is the intention that the series will eventually be repeated for other towns.

The Ulster Architectural Heritage Society is a voluntary body which embraces the nine counties of Ulster, and was founded in 1967. Its main aim is to extend the knowledge and appreciation of Ulster's Architectural Heritage. To achieve this the Society has prepared a comprehensive series of booklets on the architectural heritage of Ulster. These booklets are in fact extremely thorough surveys of various towns. Like the Dublin Amenity Study they were also produced on a voluntary basis and rely very much on the help and knowledge of local residents. The Irish Georgian Society, established in 1958, has over the years achieved tremendous success in making the general public more aware of the qualities and significance of Georgian architecture and town planning. These are, of course, one of the crowning glories of the architectural heritage. The Society has been responsible for saving and restoring many important buildings which might otherwise have been demolished, and so lost for all time.

The National Trust (Committee for Northern Ireland) has been active for many years in the field of architectural conservation. They own and manage properties of architectural and historic interest, ranging from the Wellbrook Beetling linen mill in Co Tyrone, which won a Civic Trust Award, to Castle Coole, Co Fermanagh, a fine 18th century classical house designed by James Wyatt. In addition the Trust owns the villages of Cushendun Co Antrim and Kearney Co Down. Many of their buildings have been tastefully restored and are open to the general public. The Committee have an ongoing plan for the improvement of Kearney, which includes of course the retention of its character.

In association with the Ulster Architectural Heritage Society the Committee for Northern Ireland has sponsored a new Housing Association called 'Hearth'. It is intended that the Association will be involved in the restoration and rehabilitation of dwelling houses of historic or architectural merit with the eventual aim of either letting or selling them. The idea is based on the internationally famous 'small houses scheme' pioneered by the National Trust for Scotland. The first project to be tackled has been in Seaforde Co Down. This is an exciting new venture for Ireland, and could be extended to many other parts of the country, with considerable social and aesthetic benefits.

TIDY TOWNS COMPETITION

One particularly outstanding activity, however, on a country wide basis is the 'Tidy Towns Competition' organised annually by Bord Failte Eireann. It began as a modest attempt to deal with the litter problem in Irish towns before the tourist season would commence. In other words an annual spring-clean. In the beginning the main concern was to clean up litter with a view to pleasing the tourist. At that time there was little talk of community involvement, or of social and economic renewal. Various prizes were awarded and the town adjudged best was declared the National Tidy Town winner. The competition flourished beyond all expectations, from fifty-two entries in 1958, to approximately four hundred in 1964, and in 1974 there were over six hundred. When one considers the general appearance of most Irish towns at the beginning of the fifties the results have been quite staggering. At that time they were generally drab and dreary, with derelict and unused buildings, full of litter and refuse, and little outward sign of community life. The emphasis on the competition has in addition changed over the years. From an earlier concern with litter, and general tidiness, it now covers many aspects of urban renewal and conservation. There was also a tendency in the early years of the competition for local committees to over-prettify their town with flowers and fussy ornamentations, while in the same village the river may have been neglected, or an old mill or church which could have been restored was in a derelict condition. The present emphasis on the competition is now towards developing the essential character and quality of the town. Committees are asked to note certain features about their town which make it distinctive from their neighbour's. To highlight these, bonus marks are given for improvements such as restoring an old mill, improving a bridge, retaining traditional shopfronts and so on.

Some of the results in this field have been very good indeed. The fair greens in Malin Co Donegal, and Tyrrellspass Co Westmeath, both previously in a rather decrepit state, have now been restored into village greens comparable with the best English villages. Old market houses, mills, forges, and similar buildings have been restored and given a new use. The effects of the competition have also spilled over into the surrounding countryside. Many country farm houses and cottages are improving their appearances. This is particularly noticeable in areas where the neighbouring towns may be doing well in the competition. The most important result, however, is that people in general are not only more aware, and concerned about their own properties, but also with those little pieces of waste ground, that in the past were totally ignored. A new community spirit is being forged.

This new spirit has manifested itself in a number of ways. Local committees have now definite opinions as to how future development would affect the appearance of their villages. They are quite prepared to make these opinions known to the local planning authority, and to developers. One good example of such concern can be seen at Tyrrellspass, a small village in Co Westmeath. It won the National Award in 1969. There had been a long-standing aim by a group of local people to erect a memorial to former patriots. In Ireland this, of course, is a very common occurrence. The memorial was proposed for the village green. The local 'Tidy Towns Committee' was however concerned lest the memorial should be out of character with the village. They arranged discussions between the organisations involved and Bord Failte. The result is a successful piece of design, small in scale, and fitting in perfectly with the village scene. Without this concern for the overall appearance

Tobermore Co Derry - An award winner in the 'Best Kept Village' competition in Northern Ireland.

of the village green the memorial might well have been the commonplace neo-Celtic Cross surrounded by large railings, or a grouping of soldiers. The particular design is also highly symbolic. Three young children on their way to school is a more positive omen for the future than a group of 'soldiers'.

It has been estimated that approximately 30,000 people are directly involved in the Competition. They take part in numerous activities, restoring derelict buildings, cleaning the banks of canals and rivers, painting their houses, keeping their gardens in good trim, improving the approaches to towns. One of the successes has been the involvement of the school children in the competition. In some centres the school children, with the active co-operation of their teachers, have been organised into anti-litter squads and throughout the summer they can be seen going around the various towns and villages cleaning up litter wherever it is to be seen.

In the same field, but less comprehensive and widespread, is the competition for "the Best Kept Villages and Towns" in Northern Ireland, organised by the Central Garden Association. This competition started in 1957, and in 1973 one hundred and twenty towns and villages took part. In general both competitions cover the same ground, although there is more emphasis on architectural character in the South. Perhaps it will be possible at some time in the future for both competitions to merge, and run as an all Ireland competition. It is certainly a field of common concern and interest and could be a fruitful source of co-operation between North and South.

In recent years there has been a spectacular growth in the formation of local cultural and community associations. Many of these bodies are concerned with the improvement of their physical surroundings in some way or other, the preservation of trees, the provision of open space or the protection of an existing open space and the preservation of historic buildings. The spread of such organisations is indicative of a growing concern for local amenity and environmental issues. Together with the national based organisations they contain a valuable framework on which to build up a more widespread appreciation of our architectural heritage in all its aspects.

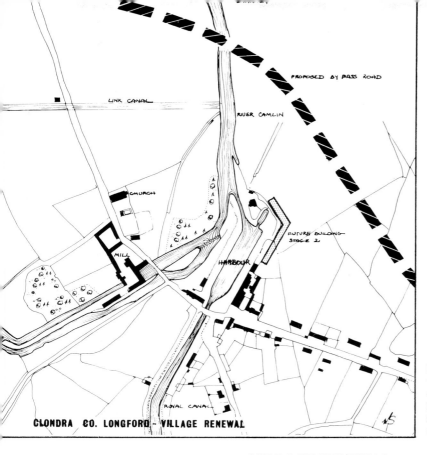

Plan of Clondra Co Longford
which shows the relationship
of the buildings to the canal,
harbour and river. However a
future by-pass will improve
the environmental quality.

VILLAGE RENEWAL

The Tidy Towns Competition has become a bye-word throughout the country. Its success has prompted Bord Failte to tackle the problems of village renewal on a comprehensive basis, taking into consideration that tourism has a social, as well as an economic objective, and that the development of tourism could be an instrument for improving community facilities. The village renewal programme is therefore principally aimed at encouraging local people to become directly involved in the restoration and preservation of their towns and villages while at the same time providing for tourist needs.

In selecting a town or village the following criteria are considered important:-

1. A volume of goodwill and initiative must exist, and the community as a body are to be fully involved in the project.

2. The town should be of sufficient character to be worthy of preservation and development and also have a definite tourist potential.

3. It should have the full backing of the local authority, and other public bodies.

The scheme is essentially a pump primer for the ultimate renewal of the entire village. The main aim is, with a limited amount of expenditure and intensive community involvement, to carry out certain developments which would enhance the character and potential of the village and immediate area.

The first village to be selected was Clondra Co Longford. Clondra, or formerly Richmond Harbour, is situated at the last lock on the Royal Canal at its junction with the Shannon. It was developed principally in the eighteenth century, its primary function was in transportation. The main boats left Richmond Harbour for Dublin — a journey of two days. One could also travel from here down the Shannon to Athlone and Limerick. Over the years, as with many other villages, its function changed and its main activities became agricultural. Neither the canal nor the river were important elements in the life of the community. However, the growing trend towards leisure time activities, and the increased popularity of the inland waterways brought Clondra into prominence again. It contains one of the few dry docks on the Shannon navigation and the harbour is a fine example of canal engineering. Both the harbour and dry-dock were recently restored by the Office of Public Works with the aid of a grant from Bord Failte.

A feature of the village is its fine stone buildings and bridges. The combination of canal-type buildings, bridges, mills, trees, all combine together to provide a pleasant and distinctive environment.

An initial survey of the village revealed that quite considerable improvements could be achieved with a minimum of expenditure. A public meeting was held in Clondra in January 1971, attended by officials of the Midland Region Tourism Organisation, Bord Failte, County Council, various local associations and many individual members of the community. The concept of village renewal was explained and it was suggested that Clondra would be an ideal choice for a pilot scheme. It became clear at this first meeting that one of the main community objectives in Clondra was the achievement of a proper water supply. The village had no piped water supply, although discussions about a group water scheme had been going on for a number of years. It did not make sense to ask a community to clean up their village and paint their houses when they lacked such a basic amenity as a piped water supply, and so it was agreed there and then that one of the first aims of the Scheme should be to help towards the provision of a water supply.

A plan was prepared which outlined the type of work to be carried out, the stages at which they would be implemented and the cost of various items. It involved the painting of facades, rebuilding derelict walls, the removal of eyesores, putting unsightly wires underground, acquiring property crucial to the longterm development of the village. The more difficult tasks such as repairing and building walls were carried out by a local building contractor. In addition and in co-operation with the County Council, an overall development plan for the village was prepared, to ensure that new developments would blend with the character of the village. A special ad hoc committee was set up which included representatives of the local community, Bord Failte, the Midland Regional Tourism Organisation and Longford County Council. This committee administered the funds available to carry out the scheme. The County Council also carried out certain works such as cleaning the river and repairing bridges. The Office of Public Works surfaced the quayside. The E.S.B. and Department of Posts and Telegraphs laid their services underground.

The initial stage was to provide the group water scheme, to acquire certain land of importance to the scheme, and the removal of the more prominent eyesores. A colour scheme was prepared and people were advised as to the type of paint colour and other matters. There was however no compulsion to

Top - Clondra Co Longford - The harbour before restoration.
Centre and bottom - Derelict buildings being removed.

A pleasant scene at Clondra after the completion of stage 1 of the renewal project, and during the visit of the Shannon Boat Rally to the harbour.

decorate a house or in fact do anything at all. The first houses in the village were painted and suddenly the local community realised that this was not just another 'pipe dream'. The first stage was completed in the summer of 1972. The Shannon Boat Rally visited Clondra in July 1972 and the restoration scheme was formally opened amid great excitement. The next stage envisages the restoration of other buildings in the village.

For a modest outlay this scheme can be considered a success in many aspects: the local community now have a better civic spirit and a greater awareness of the character of their own village. They also appear to be functioning more as a community rather than as a number of individuals. Clondra has now become more than a place on the road between Dublin and Sligo. Other people have discovered it. As a result there is a demand for new housing sites and property values have gone up. The provision of a by-pass to the village, which is likely to be in operation by 1976, will enhance these values further.

It was not all plain sailing however. Not everybody in the community co-operated, the tradition of waiting for help is still strong. It was initially difficult to co-ordinate people to act as a community rather than individuals. The small size of the village meant that there were fewer local people to act as leaders. However, Clondra has demonstrated quite forcibly that it is possible, with a minimum amount of expenditure, and with co-operation to improve the appearance of a village while at the same time providing much needed community facilities. What has been achieved in Clondra could also be achieved in other villages.

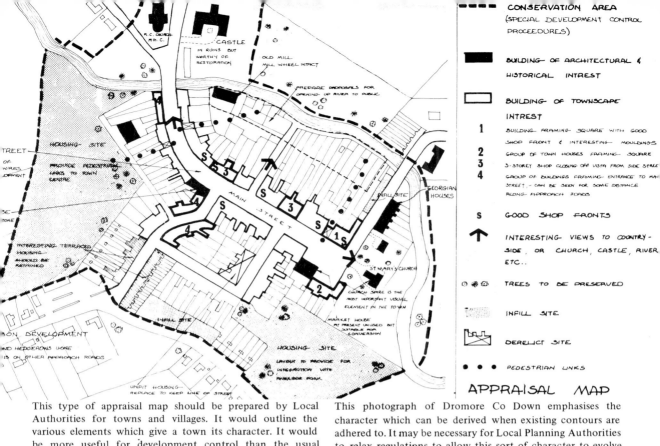

APPRAISAL MAP

CONSERVATION AREA
(SPECIAL DEVELOPMENT CONTROL PROCEEDURES)

BUILDING OF ARCHITECTURAL & HISTORICAL INTREST

BUILDING OF TOWNSCAPE INTREST

1 BUILDING FRAMING SQUARE WITH GOOD SHOP FRONT & INTERESTING MOULDINGS
2 GROUP OF TOWN HOUSES FRAMING SQUARE
3 3-STOREY SHOP CLOSING OFF VISTA FROM SIDE STREET
4 GROUP OF BUILDINGS FRAMING ENTRANCE TO MAIN STREET, - CAN BE SEEN FOR SOME DISTANCE ALONG APPROACH ROADS

S GOOD SHOP FRONTS

INTERESTING VIEWS TO COUNTRY-SIDE, OR CHURCH, CASTLE, RIVER ETC..

TREES TO BE PRESERVED

INFILL SITE

DERELICT SITE

PEDESTRIAN LINKS

This type of appraisal map should be prepared by Local Authorities for towns and villages. It would outline the various elements which give a town its character. It would be more useful for development control than the usual zoning maps.

This photograph of Dromore Co Down emphasises the character which can be derived when existing contours are adhered to. It may be necessary for Local Planning Authorities to relax regulations to allow this sort of character to evolve in the new housing areas.

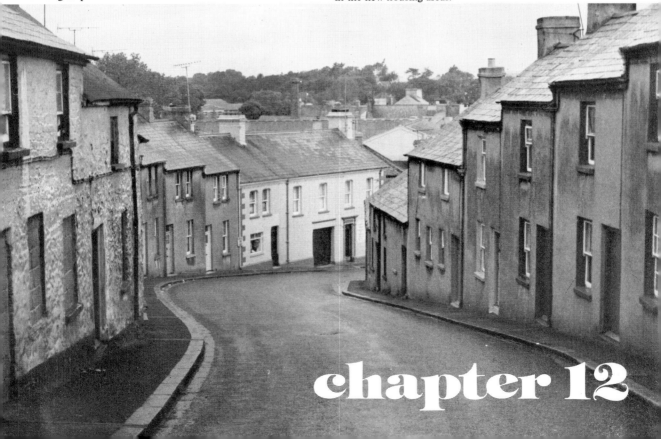

chapter 12

A Policy for Conservation (2)

THE ROLE OF LOCAL AUTHORITIES

The Planning Authorities in the first analysis hold the key to a successful policy of architectural conservation. They have behind them all the powers of planning legislation, and also the basic philosophy of planning which is intended to be in the interest of the common good. This has been emphasised in the preamble to the Local Government Planning and Development Act 1963 — *'an Act to make provision in the interests of the common good for the proper planning and development of cities, towns, and other areas, whether urban or rural, including the preservation and the improvement of amenities thereof'.*

The 1963 Planning Act in the Republic and the 1972 Planning Order in Northern Ireland both confer comprehensive powers on their respective planning authorities. In the South there are approximately 75 planning authorities ranging from urban district councils responsible for a population as small as 1,500 to those responsible for the large cities and counties. In the North the Ministry of Development is the planning authority In the South all planning authorities must prepare a development plan for their area. In the North the Ministry may prepare a plan for any area. Before adopting any plan the planning authority must ensure that the general public has been fully informed about their contents and proposals. Both Acts contain provisions to ensure full public participation in planning matters. This means first making a draft plan, then putting it on public display, and taking into account the objections and observations of local people. However, up to now, this public consultation had been carried out more to the letter of the law rather than in the spirit. Development plans have generally been prepared as legal documents, rather than to inform the general public.

In addition under the Planning Acts all developments (except certain exempted ones specifically listed in the Acts) which constitute a physical change in the appearance of a building, or a change in its use, require the permission of the planning authority. Developers whether they are a multi-national concern proposing to build a smelter, or redevelop a large part of a city or town, or, a single individual carrying out alterations to a shop or house, must all submit details of their proposals, and receive the approval of the planning authority before commencing the work. The planning authorities must decide on the application, taking into account the proper planning and development of the area and having regard to their own development plan. This process is known as development control and here the general public are also involved, particularly in the South where any person can appeal against a decision by the planning authority. This is known as a third party appeal and has given rise to considerable controversy since the Planning Act came into operation. Many developers and some Architects would like to see it scrapped altogether. They consider it allows cranks and busy-bodies to hold up valuable development projects, and that it slows down social and economic progress. However, experience to date has shown that in fact by far the greater percentage of third party appeals are made by individuals and organisations who are genuinely concerned This concern may be about the effect the development could have on an individual's property or livelihood, or, the effect it might have on the general environment of the area, and in some cases the entire country. Third party appeals are now firmly a part of the planning tradition in Southern Ireland and are likely to remain so for the forseeable future.

At present the Minister of Local Government considers and determines planning appeals, but under amending legislation now being considered, it is proposed to hand over this function to an Appeals Board. This change is being made as a result of considerable political and public pressure over the last few years to remove the decision making from the political arena altogether. In the North the general public are not involved to the same extent. The Ministry of Development as Planning Authority determines all planning applications. All applications are advertised by the Ministry in the local press. In determining the application they must consult with the local district council and also take into account representations made by any person. When the decision has been made only the applicant can appeal. The appeal is heard by an independent appeals commission.

In the field of architectural conservation however the Northern Act has stronger and more specific powers. The Ministry of Development can compile a list of buildings of special architectural and historical interest. When a building is listed any work of development, alteration, extension or demolition is subject to special control procedure. To carry out such work without permission a person would be liable to heavy fines. The Ministry has special powers to make grants or loans available for the improvement of listed buildings. Listed buildings can also be acquired by agreement or if necessary by compulsion, the Ministry can then hand over any building acquired to suitable organisations such as the National Trust for Northern Ireland. The Act also allows the Ministry to designate areas of special architectural or historic interest.

In the South there is also provision for preserving buildings of architectural, historic or artistic merit, but this is not specifically emphasised in the Act. The special emphasis, if any, has been in relation to areas of natural amenity and scientific interest. The Planning Authorities can include objectives in the plan for the preservation of important buildings. They can also include regulations for controlling the design, colour and materials of buildings. Local planning authorities have powers to make financial contributions and give technical assistance to help the preservation of buildings of architectural and historic interest, but to date little has been done in this area.

The types of buidlings listed for preservation have been restricted mainly to archaeological remains, medieval and georgian buildings. However in recent years An Foras Forbartha at the request of certain local authorities are compiling more extensive lists of buildings of architectural importance. These include market houses, courthouses, small groups of houses and other buildings, many previously overlooked, and in the future they may be included in development plans. There is no procedure whereby local planning authorities can make conservation orders in respect of areas of architectural and townscape importance. This is a power which is urgently required in the South. There is nevertheless in both parts of Ireland a comprehensive administrative framework to ensure that developments do contribute to the architectural quality of towns rather than take away from it. Planning authorities therefore must take a large amount of blame for the generally poor standard of urban design and architecture which has been carried out over the past decade in our towns and villages.

It is important to remember that practically all the bad developments that we can see around us in our towns and villages, have in fact received planning permission in some form. Either from the local authorities or through the appeals system. Apart from the classical georgian areas of Dublin it is almost unheard of for a development to be refused on aesthetic grounds. On the other hand it is quite common for a refusal to be based on lack of car parking, inadequate road width, unsuitable uses and so on.

In Ireland planning is a new concept. When the 1963 Planning Bill became law there was no tradition for and little experience of physical planning. The number of adequately trained planners was very few indeed. Professional staff were drafted in from other activities in the local authority and asked to assume responsibility for planning. Planning was considered as just another technical problem similar to services and roads. The status of the planner in local government has reflected this. Apart from Dublin Corporation and Dublin County Council no other major local authority employed a town planner as a chief officer in his own right. Planning should be regarded as one of the most important activities of local authorities, there is a lot of ground to be made up – for example there is no such post as County Architect. Dublin, with its internationally acclaimed architecture, has had no City Architect for over a decade. It would of course be a far more slap happy situation if the present planning laws did not exist at all, particularly where the use of land is concerned. However after more than ten years' experience under the 1963 Act it is obvious that many improvements are needed, particularly in the field of architectural conservation.

The situation in Northern Ireland is quite different, and even though there was no comprehensive planning legislation until 1972 every county had its own county planning officer. Following the reorganisation of local government the County Councils have been replaced by district councils and planning is now administered by the Central Authority. Even so the status of the professional planner is higher, and each area has its own planning office, headed by a

Above - Beragh Co Tyrone - An aerial photograph can be a useful device for informing the general public about the character and layout of a town.

qualified town planner. Forthcoming plans in the North of Ireland will be awaited with interest. The few produced to date are quite promising and suggest a more positive approach to design matters. They are generally more informative and better produced than those in the South, which possibly reflects a greater concern for planning and the higher status of the professional planner. They must of course provide the framework for the rebuilding and renewing of those Northern towns whose central areas have been so badly damaged over the past few years.

Town Planning is a complex and comprehensive matter. Making a development plan, or deciding on a planning application, can have major consequences affecting individuals and the community at large. Roads, services and housing are part of the planning process, not separate entities. The planners must take into consideration visual and aesthetic matters as well as economic, social and technical issues. Otherwise planning could become nothing more than engineering development with no concern for artistic value whatsoever. This would be a grave mistake, and a poor reflection on the present generation.

It is vitally important that the skill and expertise of professional planners should be utilized and recognised. Planning is a profession in itself and should be recognised as such. The medical profession has moved on from the days when the surgeon was also the barber.

What is now required all over Ireland is for planning authorities to be more concerned about the architectural qualities of towns. This need not mean a restrictive approach to planning. Indeed the whole point of a good conservation policy is to welcome new development, with of course, the proviso that it does not destroy the character and quality of the area in which it is located. Planning authorities must be prepared to give positive and detailed guidances to the particular type of development they would welcome, with specific information relating to building materials, building lines, scale, heights, and design matters generally. This policy need not be specifically indicated in the local development plan. Perhaps it would be better not to do so as development plans have up to now been interpreted in a highly legalistic fashion. Such guidelines would form part of the additional document prepared for the guidance of developers and the general public and should be prepared in co-operation with local voluntary groups. Public discussion should be encouraged before final adoption. This would help to reduce to a minimum the amount of wrangling and disagreement which often takes place, and which leads to unnecessary delays in the processing of planning applications.

Indeed the general impression created at present is that the whole procedure of planning is a quagmire. Some planning applications have taken years to resolve, which reflects no credit on those concerned. Even with design guidelines, there will still be arguments, and a compromise will be required in many instances. Life is not so simple that a few glossy booklets will solve all problems, and aesthetic judgments are of course subjective. But it will be a compromise based on previously stated and widely held community values. Valuable time would be saved, and the number of planning appeals would be reduced — a welcome event in itself.

Developers and their professional advisers would surely welcome a new and positive approach along these lines. Local organisations would feel more actively involved in the day-to-day planning process. Such an approach can only lead to better relationship between the planning authorities and the general public. It would also contribute towards the important national objective of conserving the character of our towns and villages.

DESIGN GUIDELINES

Guidelines should be produced in the form of a booklet, illustrated by photographs, plans and sketches, and with a minimum of technical jargon. The guidelines need not necessarily commit a local authority to a specific line of action. In preparing them, they will stimulate ideas and discussions.

Policy would of course vary with the nature and size of the town, however the following list is a general guide to what might be included:

Plan Form – Natural Setting

A general description of the plan would be required and its relationship to the surrounding landscape emphasising any distinctive features in both. The larger

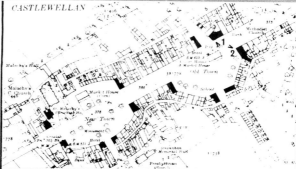

Castlewellan Co Down - A classic example of a planned town - two formal squares joined together by a wide street. The town has suffered bomb damage to important buildings. Design guidelines for this town would be likely to emphasise the importance of the corner buildings.

1 - It is hoped that the motor showroom building is only a temporary suggestion.

2 - (See plan) Opposite this showroom is an important building not apparently used but well worth preserving.

towns can be divided up into separate areas which might make for clarity of presentation. These could be the entrances, shopping streets, areas of historic or architectural importance, riverside and landscape areas, residential areas, areas requiring renewal and improvement and areas of possible future development.

Building Lines — Roof Profiles

General directives regarding building lines would be required particularly within the built-up areas picking out the buildings that are important, and explaining why. As a general rule it will be necessary to maintain existing building lines. The profile of a town may need to be explained and stressed. Aerial photographs from a particular vantage point will be more helpful than lengthy explanations. It is likely that in most towns pitched roofs will fit in better with the existing profile. Major visual elements could be highlighted. In many towns it is the church spire or tower which has helped to define its urban form. High buildings — can they be allowed? and, if so, where? What particular size and bulk should be permitted? Remember that in the majority of towns any building over five stories should be considered a high building, and might present a visual threat to the environment. In some instances, in the smaller towns and villages even a three or four storey building could be considered high.

Form of New Development

The usual regulations regarding road widths, densities, plot ratio should be for general guidance only. Certain towns may have areas that are unique in character perhaps because of topographical conditions. It may be necessary in these cases to relax regulations regarding road widths, distances between buildings and densities, to ensure that new developments respect the existing character. The guidelines could expressly state this, and so generate a positive interest.

Buildings of Interest

Buildings that are important because of location, historical associations and architectural significance should be identified and listed. The reason why a particular building is to be preserved should be spelt out, this might for example be because of its size and relationships with other buildings or it might have certain important architectural features. In areas of historic importance it should be stated whether new developments have to respect the character of the adjacent buildings either by producing similar elevations (which might only be required in rare examples) or by designing new buildings which although having a modern appearance would be sympathetic as regards building materials, scale, proportion and good design. Sketches and drawings could be used to emphasise particular points. Local authorities should not hesitate to be specific about these matters. It need not be a question of doing the architect's work. Most architects would in fact welcome positive suggestions.

Traffic

Proposals could be made for the eventual elimination of through traffic and for the pedestrianisation of certain streets. This may generate public controversy, perhaps from the local business community reacting against a by-pass or the closing of a street. On the other hand it may be a group of local residents worried about the effect of through traffic as a hazard for themselves and their children. All the more reason therefore for public discussion on positive proposals.

Fabric and Materials

The materials used in a building or development can often mar or make it as a good piece of architecture. There are a wide variety of building materials now in common use. It is vital that planning authorities should have clear opinions as to their use. It is particularly important in the more sensitive areas of architectural quality where the wrong use of building materials could have a lasting and damaging effect. The dominant and often traditional building materials which make up the fabric of a town should be clearly identified and explained. The general range of new materials which would be considered appropriate for new buildings should be specified. It may be necessary to refer to existing developments as examples of what to avoid, and also to draw attention to the successful use of materials. As a general rule restraint in the use of materials is more successful aesthetically, as well as being less costly. In areas of high architectural quality, whether they are to be found in this country or any other, in old or modern areas, one common theme is invariably found, and that is a general restraint in the use of materials. Stone or brick might still be used in older areas and concrete or glass in modern schemes, but if restraint is practised, the visual and aesthetic quality of towns could be improved.

Interesting building characteristics such as specific use of materials in bridges and walls, and other architectural details peculiar to a town, should be highlighted by means of photographs and sketches and brought to the attention of the public. In this way many fine and distinctive local traditions can be retained and carried on for the future. Local building methods and traditions can often be incorporated into a modern building, in a modern manner.

We illustrate various aspects of towns where design guidelines would be a positive help towards better development.

1. The Quays Dublin - The treatment of the river front is extremely important to the architectural quality of Dublin The important considerations are to retain the existing street lines, general height of the buildings and the variation in detail design. Unnecessary setbacks, high buildings, long repetitive slab blocks, would all equally destroy the character.

2. Buildings such as this should be referred to, in order to avoid future mistakes.

3. The views from a town onto the surrounding countryside can be pleasant and satisfying as in Rathfriland Co Down.

4. The buildings at the ends of streets which close the vista are important, as in Ramelton Co Donegal.

5. Draperstown Co Derry - This pleasant street frontage is important to the character of the town. This point is worth emphasising, and it might avoid insensitive development similar to what has already taken place further along the street at the corner.

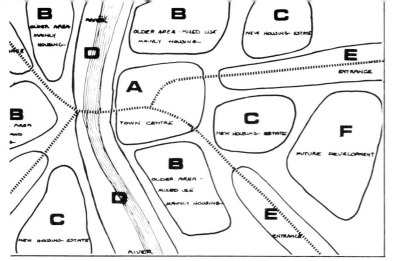

Diagram shows how larger towns could
be broken up into different areas for
the purpose of preparing design
guidelines.

The diagram contains the following labels:

B — OLDER AREA MAINLY HOUSING

B — OLDER AREA - MIXED USE MAINLY HOUSING

C — NEW HOUSING ESTATE

D

E — ENTRANCE

A — TOWN CENTRE

C — NEW HOUSING ESTATE

F — FUTURE DEVELOPMENT

B — AREA AND

B — OLDER AREA - MIXED USE MAINLY HOUSING

D

E — ENTRANCE

C — NEW HOUSING ESTATE

RIVER

Scale

This is an important, but complex matter. In Irish towns the buildings are small in scale and generally have vertical proportions. This comes from the small size of building plots, the narrow frontages and the vertical emphasis of the windows and spaces between the windows. New development with an unduly horizontal emphasis can disturb the existing composition. Where existing buildings are being re-developed the retention of the existing relationship between window and wall is desirable. With new buildings it is more difficult to be precise. Local authorities may have to rely on discussions with the developers and their architects. There may be examples locally emphasising one point or other, and these can be referred to.

Landscape

Trees that have particular visual importance should be noted and preserved, if necessary by formal tree preservation orders. Existing open spaces and other natural amenity features such as rivers and parks should be highlighted. Suggestions should be made for a gradual integration of all open spaces into a continuous and comprehensive system. The derelict areas, dumps and so forth, should be identified. Proposals should be made for clearing away these unsightly areas, and suggestions should be made as to how the derelict properties may be improved. If such areas are extensive it might be possible by means of a more comprehensive scheme to suggest a useful addition to the town, perhaps another square or open space.

Street Furniture, Road Signs

A policy to improve the design and appearance of street furniture will be required, for example the removal of overhead wires and poles and the re-arrangement of existing road signs. This will require the co-operation of several public bodies. In some cases this may even entail criticism of the local authority itself and other public bodies. If all suggestions and criticism are made in a positive and helpful way it need not cause acrimony. Perhaps as a start an attempt might be made to tidy up a certain part of the town, the results from this could stimulate efforts in other parts of the town. Stringent control of advertising will be required, with a definite idea as to where hoardings and signs will be allowed, and also what size and general design they should be.

chapter 13

Conservation~does it pay?

In the modern world, money determines many matters. Conservation policies are often in the final analysis evaluated against the resources available for them, and the returns they may make. To many people this is an unfortunate state of affairs and in the long run will prove to be a short sighted policy. There are different opinions expressed with regard to conservation — 'conservation is alright but not just to-day, let's wait until tomorrow', — 'conservation can prevent progress' — 'A developing country requires above all else a programme of economic expansion. Wealth must first be created before it can be diverted to such ephemeral subjects as architectural conservation'. These indeed are pertinent and relevant questions which conservationists must be aware of, and understand.

It is not long since central and local authorities considered that too much emphasis on conservation could frighten off investment. Developers for their part were more than happy to play this tune. Sometimes there was the suggestion or veiled hint that if planning permission was not forthcoming, and particularly a permission which would return the maximum profit irrespective of the quality of development, they would move to another town or another country. One important aim of a conservation policy must therefore be to establish that conservation is good value for money and that there are sound, tangible and obvious social and economic reasons for such a policy.

Conservation is not just a hobby; a do-good effort which a nation can afford to indulge in when it has made progress in other things. After all it is usually economic development that causes pollution. The blind pursuit of economic aims only oblivious of other needs and objectives, can create a situation where eventually there will be little left to preserve or conserve. Fortunately in modern society with the growing emphasis on the physical environment, even economic development will slow down unless there is a simultaneous policy for conservation. There is now a worldwide concern for the quality of life and for a better total environment for everybody. This hopefully will lead to a beautiful countryside, less pollution, and the protection of flora and fauna. It should also result in towns that are safe and pleasant places to live in, where the best areas are retained and renewed, where the new

Page 169 - The Old Shambles at Hillsborough Co Down
which has been successfully converted into an art centre.

170

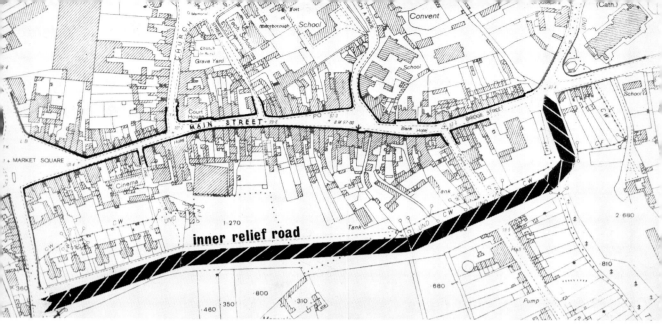

Portlaoise Town - The inner relief road has greatly improved the environmental qualify of the main street, without affecting its business potential in any way.

buildings, although expressions of our age and civilisation, respect the quality and character of the older buildings and areas. This book was an effort to show that there is no contradiction between social and economic development and a positive policy of conservation, and that even the smallest village can and should have a conservation policy.

There are a number of fields where a positive conservation policy will bring direct economic benefits.

Tourism

One of the features of modern life is the growth of tourism, and leisure time activities. In Ireland's case tourism is a major industry. Tourism to-day is however a highly complex activity, and no longer is it a matter of 'The Grand Tour' undertaken by a few privileged members of society. To-day everybody is a tourist whether it is the average Irish person on a jaunt to Britain or the Continent, or his British and Continental colleagues on a similar visit here. Tourism is also highly competitive. The would-be traveller is bombarded with a series of choices and the development of tourism is becoming essentially a marketing process. What is usually sold to the prospective visitor is the way of life and the environment of a particular country. Not only the major cities, the areas of outstanding natural beauty, the recreational activities, but also the appearance and architectural character of towns and villages and the facilities to be found in them.

Tourists and visitors are attracted to pleasant towns, and it would indeed be a hard sell in a situation where our towns and villages were losing their regional identity, where old buildings were needlessly destroyed, where new buildings were crude and unimaginative, with an appearance totally foreign to their locality. Therefore the implementation of a positive and imaginative conservation policy will certainly not hinder economic progress particularly as regards the tourist industry.

171

There are examples which emphasise this point. Kinsale Co Cork, is a town which over the past ten years has been one of the major tourist centres in the country; it is a favourite place for second homes, and for retired persons to live in. Over this period the local economy has improved out of all recognition. Property values have quadrupled in many cases, and are way above the average for other similar sized towns. People have been attracted to Kinsale, not only because of its specific location and natural beauty, but also because of the quality and visual charm of the town itself. The architectural character of Kinsale is one of its major selling points. This has been generally retained, but there are some recent examples of mediocre and vulgar development, which, if allowed to continue, could ultimately ruin the character of this beautiful place and at the same time put a stop to its economic development.

The development of the Shannon is another example of a major tourist and recreational resource that has contributed to the economic and social prosperity of the country, and in particular to the towns situated on it. In Clondra Co Longford, mentioned previously, the property values have increased significantly because of the village renewal project.

In many of the major tourist cities in Europe the principal attraction is undoubtedly the architecture, and Venice, Florence, St Malo, Dubrovonik, Bath and a host of others spring to mind. This is recognised by the cities concerned and strong conservation policies are adopted. In some cities and towns all new building must conform to those existing, and strict control is exerted over design and materials. Architectural conservation is a part of the economic life and there is little debate about this. Some towns were completely rebuilt after the war, St Malo in Brittany for example. Its historic core was destroyed during the Normandy Campaign. It was however rebuilt stone for stone in its original form. To-day it is one of the major tourist attractions in France.

One of the principal characteristics of Dublin is its architectural quality. The eighteenth century georgian streets and squares are a prime tourist attraction. The eighteenth century central. core, (still largely intact despite all its problems), the bay around which the city has, up to recently, gracefully developed, and the mountains literally at its back door, closes the vista of some city centre streets. The combination of these priceless assets gives Dublin a unique and distinctive quality which few capital cities have. If major developments were allowed to destroy the character and identity of Dublin the city would lose financially as well as culturally.

The georgian buildings have become very popular as offices. The strong conservation policy adopted by the Corporation has improved the situation, and, instead of deterring many professional and commercial organisations, has attracted them. Indeed the financial success of the conservation policy has created certain social problems as residential uses are being pushed out because they cannot compete in a market such as this.

Tourism, however, can also do damage to the architectural heritage. Its growth brings demands for new developments of many sorts. It generates increased traffic in towns and historic places. Tourism has also an in-built tendency towards conformism. Many promoters still appear to consider that the tourist is looking for a mirror image of his own culture, or, and this is just

Above - In many towns there are a variety of old disused buildings which could be converted into houses, shops, or offices, or used as a community centre. All it needs is initiative on the part of local groups, with the enthusiastic backing of the Local Authority.

An obsession with rules and regulations should never be used to hinder such developments.

Left - Restaurant in Cashel Co Tipperary - A new use for an old church.

Below - Ballyjamesduff Co Cavan - The economic base of the town, as well as its visual appearance, has improved considerably following its success in the Tidy Town's Competition.

as bad, a jazzed up version of "stage Irishery". Such pressures must be controlled. All over the world the relationship between tourism and conservation is appreciated. In November 1973 at a major conference held in Copenhagen it was accepted that tourism has become a major force in the life of Europe, of great significance in the education of its people, and that it is making an ever-growing impact on its economy and environment. The conference recognised that Europe's natural, scenic, and architectural heritage is an important element in the quality of life and a major attraction for tourism, but is also under threat from many quarters.

Housing and Traffic

In the larger towns and cities the older residential areas have become very attractive to a wide range of people. Their attraction lies in the general quality of the surroundings, and they are closer to social and community facilities. Even small artisan cottages are now fetching big prices. Some of these older residential areas have serious traffic problems as mentioned previously. If these could be alleviated then it is certain that the property values would increase even further.

The traditional view of a by-pass road or the pedestrianisation of a shopping street has been that it will cause financial hardship. The actual results are completely different. In Dromore Co Down, and Lisburn Co Antrim, the by-pass roads have not resulted in any economic losses. Trade has not declined. With the absence of through traffic, particularly the heavy lorries, it is easier and more pleasant for local people to shop and go about their business.

Trade in Main Street Portlaoise has also improved since the town relief road was opened. The pedestrianisation of Henry Street Dublin, or Market Street Tralee, did not affect trade. In Newtownards Co Down, the central square is to be pedestrianised when the security situation eases. There has been no objection to this by the local traders. The demand for housing sites and the value of existing property have increased considerably in Kill and Johnstown, Co Kildare, since both villages were by-passed. Exact economic comparison is difficult, but generally the commercial interests have welcomes the by-pass.

Industry

Industrial development is another feature of modern Irish society. There is a need for new employment to absorb the drift from agriculture and to create a more diversified economy. Various means of attracting industry have been used in the past — tax rebates, grants, cheap sites, a plentiful supply of labour. As in the case of tourism, industrial promotion is essentially a marketing process. While the emphasis may be different from tourism, the agencies involved in this field are discovering that more and more emphasis is being placed on the quality of life and the physical environment. This is true as regards certain types of industries, particularly the smaller and often labour intensive ones which are more flexible as regards location. These do not depend on specific sites such as the estuaries, and deep water ports.

Industrialists, like anybody else, are attracted to towns of charm and character. The old saying 'where there is muck there is brass' is not true any more. A dirty and untidy town with derelict buildings and sites, and shoddy architecture, is not the most attractive thing to sell to a prospective industrialist. Even when the precise location of new industry is dictated by specific needs, for example water and services, the employees and management have a much wider choice in buying or building a house. Present experience strongly suggests that in these cases they are attracted to the more pleasant towns in the locality. It is now accepted that more than mere grants and taxes are needed to attract industry to a specific area. Promoters are aware that chief executives and, just as important, chief executive's wives, can be attracted to a pleasant town. This may suggest to them a hard working community.

The example of Ballyjamesduff Co Cavan comes to mind, it is a small market town with a population of about seven hundred. In 1964 it had nothing more than the monthly fair as the centre of its economy. At that stage even the fair itself was declining.

In 1974, after winning the 'Tidy Towns Competition' on two occasions, it has five small but prosperous factories, a good hotel, and a developing economy. There is obviously more to its success than merely winning the 'Tidy Towns Competition', but there is undoubtedly a relationship between its improved social and economic situation and its visual appearance.

The Lee Maltings Cork City - The Maltings, an outstanding example of industrial architecture, was acquired by University College Cork and successfully converted for use as science laboratories, sports centre and concert hall.

The work has been commented on by Peter Dovell in his little book on Cork. "Possibly the most interesting industrial building in Cork, it is now an example of rehabilitation and conservation work at its best. Internally the spatial organization has been adroitly manipulated for its new use, and the retention of the existing scale and bold character is delightfully handled. The roughcast exterior finish is excellent, with simply but crisply articulated|slightly projecting window frames. It is a credit to all concerned, and a primer for others engaged in similar work in the city."

175

St. John's Square Limerick - This architecturally important square is being restored jointly by Limerick Corporation and private interests. Provision is being made for small professional offices and flats for students and small family groups. The old church is being restored as a museum, shop fronts and houses are getting a face lift, and eventually traffic will be removed. The scheme began as a project for European Architectural Heritage Year 1975. Of course it has a wider significance. There will be positive social and economic benefits from the venture.

It is not however just to please the tourist, to attract more industry, or to make more money that should stimulate a society to care about the quality of its towns. There are more important social and cultural reasons, that may be less tangible and seem less attractive but without them conservation would be a hollow concept indeed.

As illustrated in this book there is a rich variety of towns on the island of Ireland. They vary considerably in appearance and represent different traditions and values. They are as much a part of our cultural and historical heritage as the other aspects of Irish life more frequently emphasised, such as language, music and political aspirations. Our towns have evolved gradually, some are a thousand years old, others much younger. They are a vivid and tangible expression of our way of life, and are a link with the buildings, craftmanship and social attitudes of past generations. They provide living evidence of local skills and local identities. They are also the personification of to-day's society, the way we care for, expand and develop our towns reflects our attitudes, and this will be seen by future generations.

It is possible that Ireland could become economically prosperous, solve its many problems, but in the process destroy all that is pleasant and attractive in its towns. If this were to happen, the result would be a shallow and blinkered society.

Now is the time to embark on a national policy of architectural conservation. It is not an insurmountable problem, as this book attempted to show. It does not demand great financial investment, but it does require imagination, care, understanding and appreciation. Our society would be a happier and healthier one with such an outlook.

176

Town Trails ~ an approach

GENERAL POINTS

1 Every town is different, so every town trail should be formulated to suit the particular location. The larger town will need a more complex and varied approach, and indeed might have a number of trails relating to different parts of the town.

2 The main emphasis of a town trail is on the acquisition of knowledge and information by the participants themselves, which will lead to a better and more personal understanding and appreciation of the town. The distribution of detailed information to the participants is not necessary or desirable.

3 A series of clues or guidelines will be enough solely to stimulate ideas, and to suggest an approach to a particular aspect. Remember it is a form of exploration to discover a new world, perhaps hidden for many generations, although always there for anyone to discover.

4 The trail can vary in emphasis depending on whether it is being followed by children or adults.

5 A trail may relate in general terms to the character of a town or to more specific aspects; industrial buildings, public buildings, housing, or the natural items; rivers, trees, landscaping, or to the incidental items which make up the fabric; the building materials, architectural details, doorways, windows, name signs, lettering, footpaths, the curiosities, pumps, holy wells, shrines and follies.

6 The social and economic history can be included, and the persons responsible for designing and building the original town, and perhaps the famous or unusual persons associated with it

7 Above all else, however, a town trail should be tackled in an analytical and questioning manner. Participants should do more than merely collect information, although this is a useful exercise in itself. They should be concerned with questions such as: What gives the town its character? What makes it different from other towns? Does it stem from the character and quality of its buildings of different styles, periods and designs? Is it the layout of the streets, spacious and wide, or intricate and interesting? Is there a relationship with some major natural feature — river, parkland, mountains, coast or countryside?

As each smaller town can be appreciated under these headings, so can an individual area of the larger towns and cities.

Problems: Has the town any special problems and can they be remedied? Do they affect the town's intrinsic quality? Is it a question of insensitive modern buildings, the destruction of important buildings and of details important to the character of the town — shopfronts, lettering, architectural details? Or are the problems of general decay, dereliction and untidiness? Is there a need to remove slums and renew obsolete areas? Is the town suffering from traffic problems? Are the traffic problems arising from purely local traffic, or are they caused by through traffic because the town is situated on a busy road?

In preparing a town trail care should be taken to ensure that the selected route will not disturb property owners or infringe on privacy.

PROCEDURES

1 Route Planning: A trail should be mapped out beforehand by the trail leader and he should prepare a series of notes, suggestions, questions, and other hints all designed to involve the participants as fully as possible in the trail, and in an individual manner. It is important that the trail leader is familiar with the town, and it will be necessary to go over the trail beforehand. An examination of aerial photographs, or, better still, a view of the town from a suitable vantage point, nearby hill or church steeple, will highlight in a clear way many points not immediately observable from the ground.

2 Talk: A preliminary talk could be organised, emphasising: (a) The procedures to be adopted by the participants (b) General points of interest about the town. This talk could be given by a local architect, engineer, planning officer, teacher, historian or indeed any interested person who is prepared to act as a trail leader. The talk could be illustrated with slides or by reference to ordnance survey maps, documents, aerial photographs, old photographs and newspaper cuttings.

3 Start of Trail: The trail should lead from one focal point to another along streets and pathways which can be called linking routes, for example from the centre of the town to the country, or vice versa. In a larger town it could run from a square or public place to another square, from one public building to another, or from the centre to the riverside. Participants may work individually or in groups.

4 End of Trail: The trail of course need not be completed in one journey. It can be built up over a period and returned to from time to time. Some of the information required may need special research, in libraries, from newspapers and reference books.

5 Equipment Needed: Plans and maps showing the route. These would be arranged beforehand and would incorporate a number of questions and hints Other equipment would vary of course with the individual participants and the intensity of the trail. It may include pencils, sketching pads, camera, tape recorders, binoculars.

178

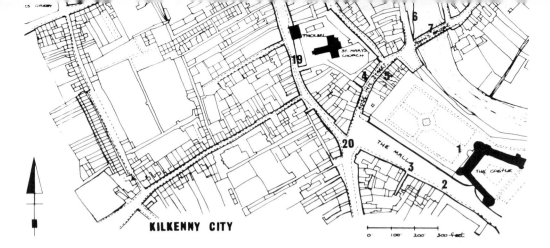

KILKENNY CITY

a trail for kilkenny

Numbers in brackets refer to photographs and map

Starting Point: An ideal starting point for a town trail of Kilkenny would be the parapets of the Castle. From here there is a fine view over the city.

Castle and Mall: Enter the castle from the Mall and examine the Castle grounds and buildings. **(1)**

Identify some of the trees and shrubs. What can you find out about the history of the Castle? Did you ever visit it before? Do you know what it is being used for at the moment? Examine the restoration work being carried out. Is it consistent with the character of the building;

Draw a few of the architectural details — gates, railings, doors etc.

Kilkenny Design Workshop: Across the road from the Castle are the Kilkenny Design Workshops. **(2)** They were formerly the stables attached to the Castle. Walk around the Workshops. Do you like the way the restoration is being carried out?

Can you think of other similar buildings in Kilkenny where a suitable restoration job could be tackled? What use would you put for these buildings?

Look closely at the details in the Workshops — quoin stones, the arched windows and doors. Sketch, draw or photograph a window or door.

Examine the trees in the Mall. What species are they? Are any of them damaged?

Are any in danger of dying? The Mall is at present being used extensively for car parking, do you think this is a good idea? What other use could you suggest for it?

Note the fine 18th century houses in the Mall. How many are still being lived in? Note also the details and the different treatments to the various front doors.

Lahert's Garage **(3)** has been vacant a long time. As a building it is out of place in this fine space. Sketch the kind of building you would like to see replacing it.

Have you any views on the location of the public toilets?

At the end of the Mall there are a number of new shop fronts, do you think they add to the character of Kilkenny?

Rose Inn Street: Walking down Rose Inn Street note the telegraph poles and overhead wires. This problem occurs throughout the City, can anything be done about it?

Note the pleasant group of shop fronts beside the supermarket. Compare these traditional designs with some of the newer shop fronts. Which do you think contributes more to the character of Kilkenny?

Look up the small alley-way on the left towards St Mary's Church.

St. Mary's Church: Visit St. Mary's Church.

What do you know of its architectural style and its history? Is it still in use? Sketch or take a photograph of the church. Suggest ideas for improving the grounds of St. Mary's.

Rose Inn Street: Continue down Rose Inn

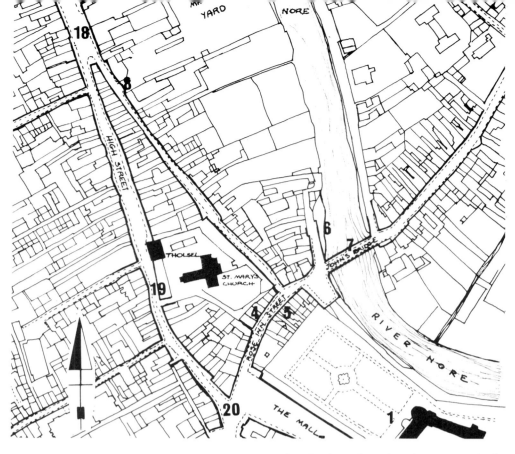

Street. Note the Shee Alms House (4). What use would you suggest for it? It is one of the few remaining medieval town houses in Ireland, therefore it is of national significance. Find out about its history.

Notice the different types of lettering on the traditional shop fronts. (5) Can you identify the types of alphabet? Could you use this lettering in your school work?

Rose Inn Street is badly affected by traffic, do you think there is a case for restricting traffic? Suggest ways in which this might be done.

Which of all the shop fronts in Rose Inn Street do you like? Sketch or photograph it. Which do you dislike most?

John's Bridge: Examine the plaque on the bridge.

What do you think of the advertisement sign on the building beside the bridge?

What suggestions would you have for improving the river banks and making them more accessible to the public? (6)

Is the river polluted? If so, what is the cause? Can it be prevented? The river effec-tively divides the city in two and the buildings on the corners act as entrances to each part of the city. (7)

There is a dilapidated area beside Tynan's Pub. Can you suggest a new use for this? Compare the design of Tynan's Pub with some of the newer lounge bars in the city.

St. Kieran's Street: There are many old buildings along this street. Should they be restored? Or should they be pulled down and the street widened to improve traffic? If they are to be restored what use could you find for them?

What do you think of the street improve-ment below St. Mary's Church?

Note the various types of doors and windows and, in fact, how all the houses on this street are different. Some are well maintained. How many are still being lived in? Are there any advantages or dis-advantages in living in a street like this? Sketch the house you like best.

If the new road as proposed along the river is built, it might be possible to pedes-trianise this street, what would you think of this suggestion?

Look up an old street directory and discover the uses in this street a hundred years ago. (This could also be done for other streets in the city). How many of them still remain?

Kytler's Inn is an example of a restored building, do you think it has been successful. **(8)** Find out all you can about the Inn and Dame Alice Kytler.

Look back and you can see the Castle in the distance. **(8)** In Kilkenny the Castle and Churches can be seen from many parts of the city. They give the city a distinctive profile. List the places from which there are fine views of the city.

Imagine the effect a new high building would have on these views. Sketch the view you can see in your mind.

The Market Place: When was the old market laid out as a car park? Is it better to have the cars parked here than on the main shopping and residential streets? When was the last market held? Have there been any famous markets, or well known incidents associated with the market?

What happened to the entrance to the market house? Should it have been retained?

Parliament Street: Notice the old cast iron street name indicating St. Canice's Ward and St. Kieran's Street. Are there any other of these name plates still in the city? Were they made locally?

Continue along Parliament Street. What do you think of the new Bank of Ireland and Winston's Department Store? What kind of buildings did they replace? Check on old photographs, if any. Which do you prefer?

Sketch or photograph the Court House. **(9)** Could you draw a large scale detail of the colums? What is the architectural style? Visit the Courthouse.

The large advertisement sign on the gable wall has been removed in the past year or so. The setting of the courthouse is improved. List other large advertisement signs throughout the city which you think should be removed.

Wander up some of the laneways. These may have been rights of way for many hundreds of years, for example, Evans's Lane. Is there any particular history associated with it?

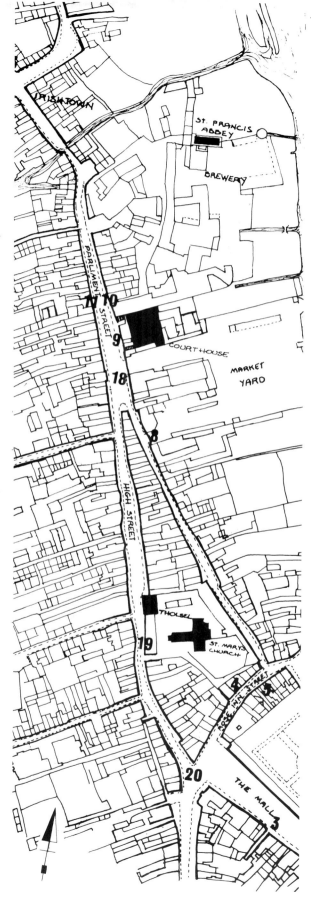

Identify the other lanes in Kilkenny. Have they any particular history?

Rothe House: Visit Rothe House.(10) (11) Compare its appearance and condition with the Shee Alms House. Do you consider it is money well spent to restore such buildings? Find out what you can about John Rothe.

Notice the fine 18th century town houses opposite Rothe House. Are these worth preserving and restoring where necessary? What is their general condition? Examine the backs, if possible. Are the doors different to other doors in Kilkenny?

Note the fine chiselled lettering on Crotty's bakery. Where else in the city do you find lettering like this? Was it carried out by a local craftsman? What can you find out about him? Did he carry out any other work in the area?

Notice how the the street bends which, in effect, marks the end of the main shopping area and imparts a certain character to the area. There are often proposals to widen street corners and improve bends in cities and towns. What do you think of this policy? Imagine this area with the bend removed.

Move around the bend and St. Canice's Cathedral lies ahead.

St. Francis's Abbey: Make a detour and visit St. Francis's Abbey and the Brewery. Are there any of the old brewery buildings still in use? Can you trace the development of the Brewery? Suggest an idea for planting some more trees at the car park beside the Brewery. Illustrate it with sketches.

Do you consider it might be worthwhile to restore St. Francis's Abbey?

Irishtown (Water Gate): Around the bend there is a small shopping centre. It has the characteristic of a distinct area. Was it ever a separate town? Has it any peculiar history of its own?

Different types of materials have been used for the footpaths, can you identify each? Where have the materials come from?

St. Canice's Cathedral: Walk up the steps towards St. Canice's. (13) This approach badly needs improvement, what would you suggest?

Visit the cathedral. (14) What do you know about its history? Was it built all at the one time? Can you identify its architecture and style? Who was responsible for the design of the various elements, wood carvings in the stalls, stained glass, etc.?

St. Canice's Cathedral was largely reconstructed in the 19th century. At that time the walls were rebuilt and the great hammer beam roof constructed. Can you find out who was responsible for this work? Was it carried out by local people? Are any of their descendants still in the building business? Where did the building materials come from? Sketch the Cathedral, and the various details. Examine the tombstones. Are any famous people buried or commemorated here? How many families and names do you recognise? How many of these names are to be found in the city?

Note the rather unfortunately sited lighting standard at the main entrance. Can you suggest another approach to this particular problem of street lighting?

St. Canice's Church (15): Coming back from St. Canice's the Tholsel clock, St. Mary's Cathedral and the Castle can be seen in the distance, sketch or photograph the view. Identify other buildings and areas you can see.

There are many derelict areas around this part of the city, can you suggest a use for them?

Abbey Street: Are the old warehouses still in use? When were they built?

Note the spire of St Mary's Cathedral in the distance.

Do you know the name of the river and bridge? Sketch the bridge? Where does the river rise? Are there any settlements on its course. Note how the sides of the bridge have been built up. They obscure the view.

The Black Abbey Church: Find out about the Black Abbey Church, its history, architecture and traditions. **(16)** Note the differences in the window design and find out the reason for this. Draw a plan of the Church.

Which of the Kilkenny churches is the oldest?

Note the new Christian Brother's School. What do you think of its architecture?

It has been suggested that the group of cottages beside St. Mary's Church be demolished and the area opened up to form a square. Do you think this is the best approach? If not, suggest an alternative. Could you draw a plan of a cottage? Sketch a doorway.

Walk back towards Parliament Street and Irishtown. How old is the wall on the right hand side which is heavily buttressed? What is the significance of the arch? Is there any history associated with it? **(17)**

What do you suggest should be done with the old buildings and walls in this area? Notice the small stones used for building some of the wall. Could you find out why they were used?

The bakery was built in 1902. What other event took place in Kilkenny that year? Are there many gate names along the road?

Back in Parliament Street — were the iron railings made locally?

High Street: Walking back along High Street the single storey shops look out of place in the centre of a city. Why is this? Do you think they should be built up higher?

Note the plaque indicating when the High Street was widened in 1880 through the efforts of John Hogan. Did any other important activities take place that year in the city?

What would you suggest for the gap site in the High Street. Sketch your ideas.

Which of the new shop fronts do you prefer? Look at the upper facades, they vary in details; have you noticed them before?

Kilkenny Arcade, the Bank of Ireland and Winstons are typical examples of modern architecture. Do you think this particular style should be extended throughout the city? **(18)**

The Tholsel: Sketch its elevation. **(19)** Who was the architect? When was it built?

The sign writing on the gable wall of Good's shop is quite bold. Would you prefer this approach to the neon signs or plastic lettering?

The dentist's house is unusual in being set back from the street. Who originally lived in this house? Why was it set back?

Look at Paul's Ltd. Note how the horizontal windows destroy the street line. Notice all the small variations in the street line which add to its interest.

Which building, apart from the Tholsel, in High Street do you prefer, and why? Make a sketch of it. Which do you dislike the most, and why?

Note how the aluminium lighting standard is fixed on top of timber poles. Do you consider this a satisfactory way of improving the street lighting? What other way would you suggest?

Look at the signs attached to the Allied Irish Banks and the Bank of Ireland buildings. **(20)** What kind of signs have they replaced? Do you consider the new signs appropriate for these buildings, if not, what do you suggest? Can you suggest another way for banks to indicate their presence, and do they need to?

This is not the only trail that could be prepared for Kilkenny. Many items have been left out, and, of course, there are other parts of the City which could be included.

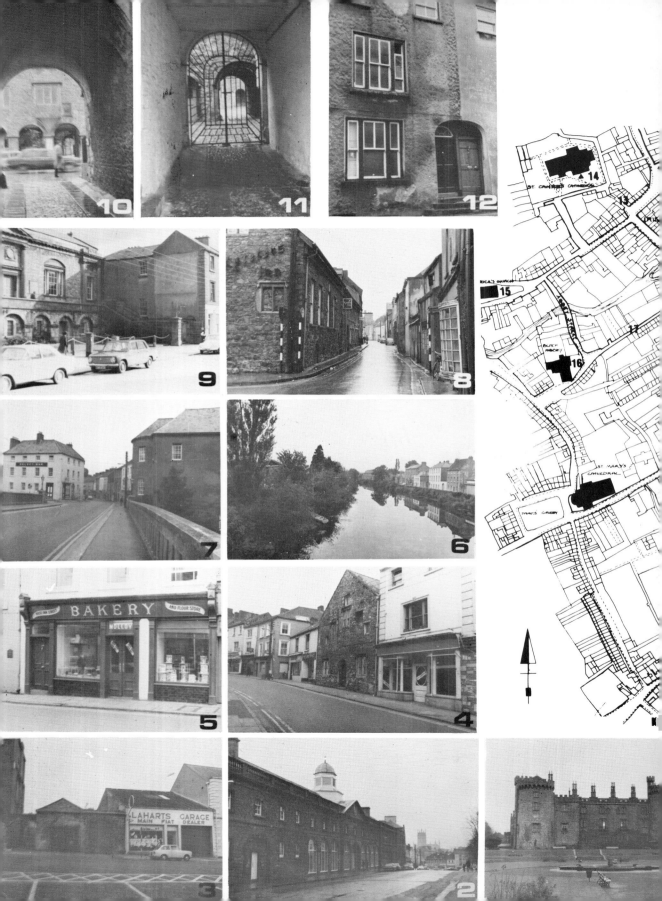

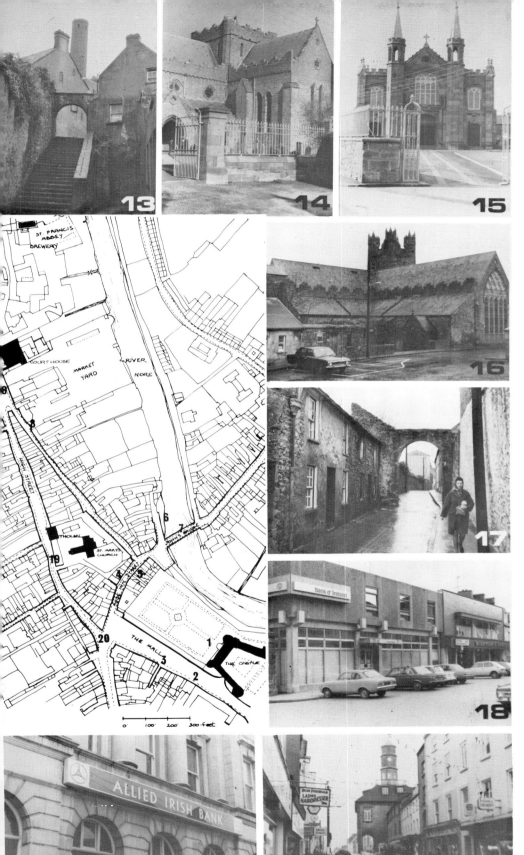

185

Glossary of Terms

By-Pass: A new road which effectively removes all the through traffic from a town or village.

Conservation: The retention only of the essential character of a building, group of buildings or specific area of a town or city. Conservation, therefore, may involve new buildings which harmonise with the old and respect the character of an area, particularly as regards scale, height, proportion and materials used.

Conservation Areas: Conservation areas are declared by Local Planning Authorities in respect of a town or part of a town which has an attractive architectural character worthy of retention. They can then prepare specific policies to ensure that the character of the area is not eroded because of economic and physical development.

Design Guidelines: A series of principles prepared by a Local Planning Authority regarding the design and character of new developments.

Density: A measurement of the intensity of any particular land use. Residential density is usually expressed in houses per acre. Commercial densities are expressed in terms of plot ratios. i.e. the total floor area of a building expressed as a ratio of the total site area. A plot ratio of 2:1 means that a two-storey building can cover the entire site, or a 4-storey building on half the site, or an 8-storey building over one quarter of the site, and so on. Local Planning Authorities may stipulate maximum densities for certain areas.

Development Control: The term given to the process of assessing and adjudicating on planning applications. Development control is carried out by Local Planning Authorities as part of their function under the Planning Acts.

Development Plan: The official policy of a Local Authority regarding the future development of their area. It is usually expressed through the medium of maps and written statements.

Entrances: Those parts of a town immediately adjacent to the main approach roads.

Environment: The physical surroundings in which we live. An environment may be good or bad depending on individual local circumstances.

Infill: The process of development or redevelopment within the existing built-up area of a town.

Landscaping: Design and development of the spaces between buildings. Landscaping can be classified into two aspects:-
(a) Hard landscaping – this refers to features such as boundary walls, footpaths, pavings which generally have a hard texture and are usually composed of man-made materials.

(b) Soft landscaping – this refers to trees, shrubs, grasses and open spaces generally.

Land-Use: The use to which any particular piece of land may be put. This can vary from agriculture, industry, shopping, housing and many others.

New Development Area: A major development on what was previously unbuilt land.

Older Housing Area: Residential streets in cities and towns generally developed prior to the 1930's or 1940's.

Plan Form: The manner in which a town or village is laid out on the ground.

Planning Blight: The erosion of the social, economic and physical characteristics of an area due to a previously made decision to carry out a major development in the future. Development could refer to roads, office or residential. In the meantime there is a moratorium on all sorts of development. It affects property sales and may prevent an individual from extending or improving his property.

Preservation: The retention of the exact physical form of a building or a group of buildings, or specific area of a town or city.

Profile: The outline of a town as seen from a nearby vantage point such as a hill, tall building or church tower, or from an approach road.

Ribbon Development: Sometimes referred to as 'urban sprawl'. The indiscriminate expansion of a town along the approach roads. This usually means that all public services are unnaturally extended and access to land at the rear is cut off, and that the visual distinction between town and countryside is completely blurred.

Relief Road: New or improved road which will allow through traffic to avoid a certain part of a town or city such as a main shopping street or a residential area.

Scale: The relative size of a building or its components in relation to its surroundings.

Street Furniture: The various elements which are to be found on the streets of most towns such as lamp standards, direction signs, litter bins, seats and advertisements.

Townscape: The visual effect created by the relationship of buildings to each other and to the spaces formed by these buildings.

Visual Stop: A barrier – buildings, trees, hills, etc. – that helps to close in and complete a present scene.

Wirescape: The term usually given to the proliferation of poles and overhead wires of all sorts.

Further Reading

GENERAL INTEREST

The Anatomy of the Village, Thomas Sharp, Penguin Press London 1950.

The Character of Towns, Roy Worksett, Architectural Press London 1969.

Buildings of England, (County by County volumes), Sir Nikolaus Pevsner, Penguin Books London 1951 onwards.

The Changing Character of Irish Towns, Patrick Shaffrey, The Irish Times, Dublin. Nov 4, 5, 6 1970.

This Ireland, Elgy Gillespie, Irish Times Dublin, Feature 1974 onwards.

The Living Street, Ruari Quinn, The Irish Times Dublin Feature Series 1973-74.

A Future for Dublin, L. Wright, Architectural Press London 1975.

Cork - An Environmental Study, P. Dovell, An Foras Forbatha Dublin 1971.

Counter Attack, I. Nairn, Architectural Press London 1957.

Dublin 1660-1860 M. Craig, Allen Figgis Dublin 1952-1969.

Houses of Ireland, B. De Breffney, R. ffolliot, G. Mott, Thames & Hudson London 1975.

Lettering on Buildings, Nicolete Gray, Architectural Press London 1960.

The Liberties of Dublin, Elgy Gillespie, The O'Brien Press Dublin 1973.

Irish Heritage, E. Evans, Dundalgan Press Dundalk 1942-1967.

Ireland Observed, M. Craig and The Knight of Glin, Mercier Press Cork 1970.

Outrage, I. Nairn, Architectural Press London 1955.

Tourism & Conservation, (Report - Copenhagen Conference), European Travel Commission Dublin 1974.

Town Design, Frederick Gibberd, Architectural Press London, 5th edition 1967.

Townscape, Gorden Cullen, Architectural Press London 1961-1971

The Town in Ulster, Gilbert Camlin, Mullan Belfast 1951.

The Village in the City, N. Taylor, Temple Smith London 1973.

What Time Is This Place? K. Lynch, The M.I.T. Press Cambridge Mass. 1960.

The World's Landscapes Ireland, A. Orme, Longmans London 1970.

PROJECTS, TOWN TRIALS

Bulletin of Environmental Education (BEE), Town and Country Planning Association, 17 Carlton House Terrace, London SW1Y 5AS.

Leicester Town Trail, Keith Wheeler, Bryan Waites, Bulletin of Environmental Education, Aug, & Sept. 1972.

How to Play the Environment Game, T. Crosby, Arts Council & Penguin Books London 1973.

The Image of the City, K. Lynch, The M.I.T. Press Cambridge Mass 1960.

Streetwork: The Exploring School, C. Ward & A. Fyson, *Routledge & Kegan Paul London 1973.*

*What Happens When . . .*Series, Gerald Bell, Oliver & Boyd.

VOLUNTARY BODIES

Amenity Study - Dublin, An Taisce - National Trust for Ireland 1967;

Belfast - Central Area Pedestrian Report, Royal Society of Ulster Architects 1974.

Conservation in Action, Civic Trust for Britain 1972.

Irish Architecture - "A future for Our Heritage." Editor Patrick Shaffrey, National Committee for E.A.H.Y. 1974.

The Market Houses and Courthouses of Ulster, C.E.B. Brett, U.A.H.S 1973.

Moving Big Trees, Civic Trust 1966.

Pride of Place, Civic Trust for Britain, 17 Carlton Terrace, London SW1 1972.

Ulster Architectural Heritage Society. Survey lists on:– Antrim and Ballymena - Banbridge - City of Derry - Coleraine and Portstewart - Craigavon Omnibus - Downpatrick - Dungannon and Cookstown - East Down - Enniskillen - Glens of Antrim - Joy Street district of Belfast - Lisburn - Mid Down - North Antrim - Portaferry and Strangford - Queen's University Area of Belfast - Rathlin Island - Town of Monaghan - West Antrim. U.A.H.S. 30 College Gardens Belfast BT9 6BT (1968 onwards).

OFFICIAL REPORTS

Area Plans (Northern Ireland): Armagh - Antrim - Ballymena - Banbridge - Belfast - Coleraine - Craigavon - Downpatrick - East Antrim - East Tyrone - Fermanagh - Limavady - Londonderry - Mid Down - Mourne Country - Newry - North Down - Randalstown /Aldergrove - Tandragee - West Tyrone. H.M.S.O. Chicester St. Belfast. 1968 onwards.

Belfast Central Area, Plan, H.M.S.O. 1969

Belfast Transportation Plan Travers Morgan H.M.S.O. Belfast 1969.

Committee on Price ofBuilding Land, (Kenny Report) Stationery Office Dublin 1974.

Control of Advertisements, Department of Local Government 1967 Dublin.

Cork Traffic Study, Cork Corporation.

Central Dublin Traffic Plan (Travers Morgan) H.M.S.O. Dublin Corporation 1973.

Dublin Traffic Plan 1965 (Schaechterle), Dublin Corporation 1973

Dublin Transportation Study, An Foras Forbatha, Dublin 1973.

Local Development Plans, Local Planning Authority. Note: All Local Planning Authorities must publish a Development Plan for their area. These can be obtained locally.

New Towns Act Northern Ireland 1965, H.M.S.O. Belfast.

Local Government(Planning and Development Act) 1963, (Part of this Act is being amended by a new Bill at present before the Dail)., Stationery Office Dublin.

People and Planning, H.M.S.O. London 1969

Planning Order (1972) Northern Ireland, H.M.S.O. Belfast.

Traffic in Towns, H.M.S.O. London 1963

Design Guide for Residential Areas, Essex County Council 1973.

Thanks

Grateful thanks are due to the following who in their own way contributed to this book.

George Bagnall and Fred Quinn, Bord Failte Eireann: Brian Ferran, Arts Council of Northern Ireland: Declan Grehan and Andrew Teare, Asbestos Cement Ltd., all for backing the idea of the book. Pat Magee, Area Planning Officer, Downpatrick, and Niall Meagher, County Planning Officer Kildare, for their help and advice: Keith Wheeler and Bryan Waites, Leicester, whose pioneering work with regard to 'Town Trails' I gratefully acknowledge: The Map Room Staff, Ordnance Survey Dublin, and the Photographic Department, Bord Failte Eireann who never refused a request for help: An Taisce (The National Trust for Ireland) for co-operation and assistance: The Ulster Architectural Heritage Society whose survey lists were of tremendous benefit: The National Committee for European Architectural Heritage Year 1975 for assistance: Tomas O'Beirne who made comments on the manuscript: Ray Hester and Derek Tynan who helped out at various stages: Pat Clarke who typed, and often retyped the manuscript: Michael O'Brien who skilfully guided the book to its production.

Above all to my wife, Maura, who painstakingly prepared the drawings and sketches for the book and without whose backing the book would not have been possible. Many other people were written to, talked with and helped in various ways. Space does not permit me to list them individually, but to all I now express my grateful thanks.

This book has been published with the assistance of Bord Failte Eireann and The Arts Council of Northern Ireland.

We are grateful to the following for permission to reproduce photographs or diagrams:—
Aerofilms Ltd. 21 (top) 24 & 25 (top) 26 (ctr.) 47 (bt.) 63 (ctr.) 163: Denis Anderson (photograph Henk Sneok) 18 (ctr.): Asbestos Cement Ltd. 147 (top lt.): Bank of Ireland 119 (bt.): B.K.S. 21 (top): Bord Failte Eireann 7, 9, 12, 13, 61 (ctr.), 75 (top), 123 (ctr) 125 (top rt.) 127 (rt.), 129, 134 (bt. lt.): Donal Burke for press cutting 71: G. Camplisson 121 (bt. lt.), 147 (bt.): M. Craig 109 (No. 2): Derry Development Commission 36: Dodder Valley Association 63 (photo The Irish Times): Dublin Corporation 104 (bt. rt.): Terry Durney sketch p. 97: Department of the Environment Stormont 15 (top rt.) 65, 67: Gilbert Camlin extract from book 'The Town in Ulster' 20: Irish Georgian Society 147 (ctr.): Irish Life (photograph John McGrath) 118 (No. 2): National Library of Ireland Lawrence Collection 67 (top lt.), 71 (top) 192: Hans Matthia 173 (ctr.): Niall Meagher 105 (top): R. McKinstry 169: F.L. McAdam diagram 83: Northern Ireland Amenity Council 154: C.F.S. Newman 15 (top), 17 (top): Northern Ireland Tourist Board 35, 38 (ctr.), 45 (top lt.), 121, 125 (top) 137 (bt.): The National Trust, Committee for Northern Ireland 149: A. O'Neill 69 sketch (bt. rt.) 106: S.O.P. O'Ceallachain 103 (ctr.), 176: J. O'Connell 125 (bt.): Pomeroy Press Ltd. 49 (bt. rt.): E.G. Pettit & Co. 175: Robinson Keefe & Devane 55 (bt. rt.): P. Rossmore 109 No. 4: Smyth & McMurtry 88: Swords Community Council 69: Stephenson Gibney 112 (bt.): Carl McDonough 178: Dr. J.K. St. Joseph, University of Cambridge, 15 (bt. lt.) 23 (t. left), 26 (top) 31, 34 (top), 55 (top): Town Plans based on Ordnance Survey maps with the sanction of the Controller of Her Majesty's Stationery Office, and The Director, Ordnance Survey, Dublin: The remaining photographs are by the author.

Index to Places

Numbers in brackets refer to illustrations.

General Index

BUILDINGS GONE
∨

Armagh City: The buildings shown in the old photograph (No. 1) were for many years an important element in the Market Square of Armagh. Over the years these buildings changed little, but, unfortunately, they have now been destroyed by bombing (photograph 2).

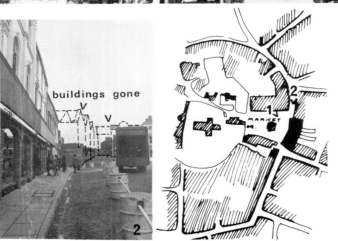

buildings gone
∨   ∨

Near yonder thorn that lifts its head on high,
Where once the sign-post caught the passing eye,
Low lies that house where nut-brown draughts inspir'd,
Where grey-beard mirth and smiling toil retir'd,
Where village statesmen talk'd with looks profound,
And news much older that their ale went round.
Imagination fondly stoops to trace
The parlour splendours of that festive place;
The white-wash'd wall, the nicely-sanded floor,
The varnish'd clock that click'd behind the door;
The chest contriv'd a double debt to pay,
A bed by night, a chest of drawers by day;
The pictures plac'd for ornament and use,
The twelve good rules, the royal game of goose;
The hearth, except when winter chill'd the day,
With aspen boughs, and flowers, and fennel gay;
While broken tea-cups, wisely kept for show,
Rang'd o'er the chimney, glisten'd in a row.

from The Deserted Village by Oliver Goldsmith.

It is important that when development takes place the design of the new buildings contributes towards improving the quality of the square. The important considerations are the individual expression of the buildings, a varied profile, and adherence to the original building line.

A final message — new development should add to the character of towns, not take away from it.

192